54.60 Africa

Femi Elufowoju jr

I0141058

methuen | drama

LONDON • NEW YORK • OXFORD • NEW DELHI • SYDNEY

METHUEN DRAMA

Bloomsbury Publishing Plc, 50 Bedford Square, London, WC1B 3DP, UK
Bloomsbury Publishing Inc, 1359 Broadway, New York, NY 10018, USA
Bloomsbury Publishing Ireland, 29 Earlsfort Terrace, Dublin 2,
D02 AY28, Ireland

BLOOMSBURY, METHUEN DRAMA and the Methuen
Drama logo are trademarks of Bloomsbury Publishing Plc.

First published in Great Britain 2025

A catalogue record for this book is available from the British Library.

Library of Congress Control Number: 2025939456

ISBN: PB: 978-1-3505-8931-5
ePDF: 9781-3505-8932-2
eBook: 9781-3505-8933-9

Series: Modern Plays

Typeset by Mark Heslington Ltd, Scarborough, North Yorkshire

For product safety related questions contact
productsafety@bloomsbury.com.

To find out more about our authors and books visit
www.bloomsbury.com and sign up for our newsletters.

arcola
theatre

54.60 Africa

By Femi Elufowoju jr

First performed at Arcola Theatre

Saturday 14th June 2025

arcolatheatre.com

020 7503 1646

Registered Charity in England, No. 1108613
Registered Address: 24 Ashwin Street, London, E8 3DL (UK)

E(ö)E
ELUFOWOJU jr
~ENSEMBLE~

54.60 Africa
By Femi Elufowoju jr

CAST

Africa 1 (Yaa Africa): Suzette Llewellyn
Africa 2, Musician: Patrice Naiambana
Africa 3: Munashe Chirisa
Africa 4, Dancer: Christopher Mbaki
Africa 5, Musician: Usifu Jalloh
Africa 6, Singer: Ayo-Dele Edwards
Africa 7: Adil Hassan
Africa 8, Singer: Funlola Olufunwa
Africa 9, Dancer, Singer: Liana Cottrill
Africa 10, Musician, Singer: Denis Mugagga
(The Ganda Boys)
Africa 11, Musician, Singer: Daniel Sewagudde
(The Ganda Boys)

CREATIVE TEAM

Director/Writer/Lyricist: Femi Elufowoju jr
Production Designer: ULTZ
Music Director/Composer/Sound Designer: Emmanuel
Edwards
Lighting Designer: Charles Balfour
Associate Director/Movement Director: Kemi Durosinmi
Stage Manager (on Book): Naomi Shanson
Assistant Stage Manager: Joe Collins
Production Manager: Joe Prentice
Dramaturg: Mert Dilek
Associate Producer: Thomas Kell (Elufowoju jr Ensemble)
Associate Designer: Mark Simmonds

**The original soundscape for this production additionally
includes the work of the following musicians:** Lánre Njoku,
Richard Olatunde Baker **and** Maurice Louis Broguitar.

ARCOLA THEATRE

Arcola Theatre, a vibrant cultural landmark in Hackney for twenty-five years, produces bold, diverse theatre, premiering new works alongside reimagined classics. As an international artistic hub celebrating voices from all backgrounds, we've launched countless careers and groundbreaking productions that challenge perspectives and inspire change. We support artists at all career stages, offering vital space to develop their craft in our two performance venues. Our affordable ticket scheme includes 'Pay What You Can' making extraordinary theatre accessible to everyone.

Our acclaimed annual Grimeborn Opera Festival showcases innovative works, while our award-winning Participation department creates thousands of creative opportunities for local communities. We provide free rehearsal space to culturally diverse and refugee artists. Our pioneering environmental initiatives aim to create the world's first carbon-neutral theatre, demonstrating our commitment to sustainability in the arts.

Arcola has received the UK Theatre Award for Promotion of Diversity, *The Stage* Award for Sustainability and the Peter Brook Empty Space Award.

ARCOLA TEAM

Artistic Director: Mehmet Ergen
Executive Producer/Deputy Artistic Director: Leyla Nazli
Finance Manager: Steve Haygreen
General Manager/Participation Manager: Charlotte Croft
Artist Associate/Producer: Katharine Farmer
Operations Managers: Catriona Tait and Carmen Keeley Foster
Marketing Coordinator: Serena Coady
Marketing Assistant: Ella Muir
Participation Coordinator: Aoife Beaumont
Production Assistant: Sadie Pearson
Technical Manager: Matthew 'Lux' Swithinbank

Supported using public funding by
**ARTS COUNCIL
ENGLAND**

Bloomberg
Philanthropies

This production is kindly supported by Linda Keenan.

54.60 Africa Team

Photography by Arcola Theatre.

THE ELUFOWOJU JR ENSEMBLE

The Elufowoju jr Ensemble was launched by Femi Elufowoju jr and Thomas Kell to gather a world-class company of multidisciplinary theatre artists whose imaginations, talents and practice are rooted in Africa.

The spark that ignited the ensemble came in 2013 with the desire to create a stage adaptation of Lola Shoneyin's novel, *The Secret Lives of Baba Segi's Wives*. Development and productions spanned the UK and Nigeria, fulfilling the aim of straddling theatre traditions across continents. With support from Arts Council England (ACE), Stratford East hosted R&D before the Arcola provided a home for the inaugural and triumphant 2018 UK production. Around the same time audiences at the Ake Festival in Lagos saw Baba Segi stride out on home soil. Subsequently Elufowoju jr re-adapted *The Secret Lives of Baba Segi's Wives* for BBC Radio Drama.

Across these years, Femi Elufowoju jr embarked on his personal odyssey across all fifty-four nations of Africa. It became clear that his experiences could fuel a new stage production. And so (despite Covid-19's unwelcome arrival) *54.60 Africa* was intensively researched and developed. Again supported by ACE, the Ensemble worked closely with Omnibus Theatre, Bernie Grant Arts Centre and Hackney Showroom to explore and share with audiences a major piece of emerging theatre. Further R&D was curated by the National Theatre's Generate programme. And now, thanks to Arcola Theatre, *54.60 Africa* – after its own extensive odyssey – reaches the stage and the audiences the company was created to serve.

The Elufowoju jr Ensemble: Our Thanks

During the long and winding process of researching and developing *54.60 Africa* for the stage we worked with and benefitted from the input and insights of many brilliant creatives, organisations and friends.

We are so grateful to:

Performers & Creatives
Michael Abubakar, Rose Aloke, Prisca Bakare, Olivia Boyd, André Bright, Munashe Chirisa, Heather Craney, Kemi Durosinmi, Ayo-Dele Edwards, Emmanuel Edwards, Elushade Elufowoju, Tyler Fayose, Sadeysa Greenaway-Bailey, Shanu Hazzan, Stephen Hiscock, Renu Hossain, Joelle Ikwa, Tunde Jegede, Aïcha Kossoko, Mark Lockyer-Shaheen, Patrice Naiambana, Richard Olatunde Baker, Camille Maalawy, Jemima Mayala, Lucian Msamati, Denis Mugagga, Karl Njoku, Lánre Njoku, Sunny Nwachukwu, Ade Omoloja, Sabrina Richmond, Daniel Sewagudde, ULTZ, Diana Yekinni, Hemi Yeroham.

Organisations
Omnibus Theatre, Clapham; Hackney Showroom; Bernie Grant Arts Centre; National Theatre Studio and the National Theatre Generate Programme; Africa Centre.

Special Friends
Dotun Adebayo, Olu Alake, Chrissy Angus, Ola Animashawun, Clint Dyer, Sophia A Jackson, Nina Lyndon, Marie McCarthy, Rufus Norris, Frank Sweeney.

We are so grateful to all the generous donors supporting our *54.60 Africa* gofundme.com campaign which was ongoing at the time of publication.

And with immense thanks to Linda Keenan who has been with us all the way and then ensured we got to our destination.

The Elufowoju jr Ensemble

Founder and Creative Director: Femi Elufowoju jr OBE
Director and Company Secretary: Thomas Kell

elufowojujrensemble.com
office@elufowojujrensemble.com
Registered in England and Wales, No. 09732116
Registered Address: Kemp House, 160 City Road, London, EC1V 2NX (UK)

54.60 *Africa* in rehearsal

Photography by Alex Brenner. (1) Femi Elufowoju jr directs the ensemble; (2) Usifu Jalloh; (3,4) the ensemble.

CAST

Suzette Llewellyn – Africa 1 (Yaa Africa)

Suzette's theatre work includes: *The Ballad of Hattie and James* (Kiln Theatre), *Foxes* (59e59 Theaters NY,NY), *The Fellowship* (Hampstead Theatre), *Electric Rosary* (Royal Exchange Manchester), *Running With Lions* (Talawa Theatre, Lyric Theatre Hammersmith), *Chigger Foot Boys* (Strongback Productions & Tara Art), *Urban Afro Saxons* (Talawa Theatre), *Marisol* (Traverse Theatre). Television and film includes: *Mr Loverman, Vera, EastEnders, Holby City, The Mouse, Doctors, Real, Top Boy, The Windsors, Faces, Hollyoaks, The Dumping Ground, Rocket's Island, Bucky, The Coroner, Scott & Bailey, Black Silk, Playing Away, Babymother* and *Welcome To The Terror Dome*.

Patrice Naiambana – Africa 2, Musician

Patrice's TV credits include: *The Witcher* (Netflix), *Criminal Record* (Apple), *Death in Paradise* (BBC), *Black Ops* (BBC), *House of the Dragon* (HBO). Film credits include: *Damsel* (Netflix), *Turn up Charlie* (Green Eyed Boy), *Spectre* (B24 Limited) and *Monochrome* (Electric Fix). Theatre credits include: *Tree* (The Young Vic), *Barber Shop Chronicles* (National Theatre), *The Caretaker* (Bristol Old Vic), *The New Nigerians* (Arcola Theatre), *Iyalode of Eti (Duchess of Malfi)* (Utopia Theatre) and *The Secret Lives of Baba Segi's Wives* (Arcola Theatre/Elufowoju jr Ensemble).

Munashe Chirisa – Africa 3

Munashe is a Zimbabwean-born, UK-based actor and comedian with a diverse portfolio across stage, film and television. His theatre credits include: *The Play That Goes Wrong* (Duchess Theatre), *New Apostles* (Young Vic), *Stop and Search* (Arcola Theatre) and *Doctor Faustus* (Tangle). On screen, he has appeared in the Bollywood feature *Time To*

Dance. Munashe is also known for his original one-man show *All of Us*. He is the co-founder of Made in ZWE, a creative platform celebrating Zimbabwean culture through performance and media.

Christopher Mbaki – Africa 4, Dancer

Christopher is a graduate of Intermission Youth Theatre. He went on to train in musical theatre with the Almeida Young Company, and then joined the National Youth Theatre in 2023. He is currently a member of Trybe House. His performance credits include *Juliet and Romeo* and *MSND* (The Chelsea Theatre with Intermission Youth Theatre), *None of the Clocks Work* (Theatre Peckham), and a national schools tour of *Shakespeare Up Close* (Orange Tree Theatre), where he played Romeo in *Romeo and Juliet* and appeared in *Macbeth*. Most recently, Christopher was nominated for a Black British Theatre Award (Best Male Lead Actor in a Play) for his one-man show *Before I Go* (Brixton House).

Usifu Jalloh – Africa 5, Musician

Usifu is an award-winning storyteller, performer, actor and educator who has worked in arts education for over thirty years. His roots in multicultural Sierra Leone and his long-standing and close association with artists and audiences from various cultures have led him to develop a storytelling style encompassing international languages, music, dance and story themes. His productions, *Africa's Cowfoot* and *The Cowfoot Prince Chronicles*, serve as platforms for promoting Sierra Leonean and African cultures by embodying them within the rich oral heritages of his ancestry. Usifu is the author of a collection of African stories, children's storybooks and a *Teacher's Handbook To Storytelling*. He has also co-written and co-published a play, *Sweet Peter*, which represents the experience of slavery, colonialism and war in Sierra Leone. His latest film/documentary *The Cowfoot Prince* is a collaboration with director Bex Singleton and the

National Film and Television School. His recent theatre roles include *The Secret Lives of Baba Segi's Wives* (Arcola Theatre/Elufowoju jr Ensemble). His latest production is *One Cowrie Shell*, an epic story Usifu developed and produced over a four-year period.

Ayo-Dele Edwards – Africa 6, Singer

Ayo-Dele is an actor and singer-songwriter. A graduate of Mountview Theatre School, she has showcased her talents across theatre, radio, film and voice-over work. Her passion for integrating music, dance and movement into storytelling led her to create her solo play, *Becoming*, which weaves narrative with original songs to explore themes of identity, relationships and migration. Currently in development for a tour, *Becoming* builds on Ayo-Dele's extensive stage experience. She is thrilled to return to the stage for this production. Her theatre work includes: *Still Breathing* (Unlock the Chains Collective, Sheldonian Theatre Oxford), *Here's What She Said to Me* (Utopia Theatre/Sheffield Theatres), *The Secret Lives of Baba Segi's Wives* (Arcola Theatre/Elufowoju jr Ensemble). *Iyalode of Eti (Duchess of Malfi)* (Utopia Theatre/West Yorkshire Playhouse).

Adil Hassan – Africa 7

Adil trained at the Guildhall School of Music and Drama, graduating in 2024.

He recently made his professional stage debut, playing Saleem in *Providers* (Brixton House). His other theatre work includes *Strangers* Makrooh (Soho Theatre) and *Deen and Dunya* (Royal Court Theatre), which he wrote. His short film work includes: *The Pilgrimage*, *DIY E.D.I* and *Can't Let Them In*.

Funlola Olufunwa – Africa 8, Singer

Funlola trained at the Royal Academy of Dramatic Art. Her work in theatre includes: *All's Well That Ends Well* (RSC), *The Time Machine* (Creation Theatre), *Sleeping Beauty* (Greenwich Theatre), *Doubt* (English Theatre of Hamburg) and *Someone of Significance* (Vaults Theatre Festival), which won the People's Choice Award in 2023. Her television work includes: *No Return*, *Emmerdale* and *EastEnders*. Her other work includes: motion capture and audio work on the *Strange Brigade* video game and writing *Keeping Up With Kassandra* for Creation Theatre's digital theatre season in 2021.

Liana Cottrill – Africa 9, Dancer, Singer

Liana's theatre work includes: *The Little Mermaid* (Bristol Old Vic) and *Wendy: A Peter Pan Story* (Bath Theatre Royal). Liana is a founding member of Bristol Old Vic's Young SixSix company, where her credits include: *Lysistrata*, *Romeo & Juliet* and *Antigone*. Beyond acting, Liana is a distinguished dancer and a key member of the renowned dance crew IMD Legion. The crew has not only dominated the UK scene as six-time reigning champions but also recently took the title of Ultimate Advanced Hip Hop World Champions 2024.

The Ganda Boys

Denis Mugagga – Africa 10, Musician, Singer

Daniel Sewagudde – Africa 11, Musician, Singer

The Ganda Boys bring a fresh light to joyous African songs and chants, with sprinklings of English lyrics by band member/lyricist, Craig Pruess. Originally from Uganda, London-based lead singers Denis Mugagga and Daniel Sewagudde are internationally recognised, with twenty-one GRAMMY artists joining their song 'The Forgotten People' in Studio City, Los Angeles. Stevie Wonder is a big fan of the Ganda Boys, appearing in public with the band during 2019.

CREATIVE TEAM

Director/Writer/Lyricist – Femi Elufowoju jr

Femi Elufowoju jr's previously written plays include *Tickets and Ties; the African tale* and *Sammy* (Theatre Royal, Stratford East), *Booked!* and *Makinde* (Oval House). *54.60 Africa* is his first published play. As a theatre director, he has served as an associate at Royal Court Theatre, Almeida Theatre, New Wolsey Theatre, Ipswich and Leeds Playhouse. Plays directed at Arcola Theatre include *The Gods are not to Blame, Blue/Orange, The Secret Lives of Baba Segi's Wives*, Best Director (OFFIE 2019), *Hoard, The Glass Menagerie* and *The Book of Grace*. Elufowoju jr was the founding artistic director of tiata fahodzi, which he led for 14 years before stepping down to pursue a freelance career. Success with the company included his Olivier-nominated production *Iya-Ile (the first wife)* by Oladipo Agboluaje. As an opera director, his works include his award-winning *Rigoletto* (Opera North) Best Opera production Sky Arts South Bank 2023, and *Der anonyme liebhaber* (Konzert und Theater St Gallen). Elufowoju jr also directs BBC radio dramas and as a performer, has extensive stage, film and television credits. He was appointed Officer of the Order of the British Empire (OBE) in the 2023 King's Birthday Honours List.

Production Designer – ULTZ

ULTZ is an Olivier Award-winning, UK Theatre Award-winning, Off-West End Award-winning, Tony Award-nominated designer based in London. He works internationally, designing and directing for opera and theatre. Previously for Elufowoju jr Ensemble and tiata fahodzi at Arcola Theatre: *The Secret Lives of Baba Segi's Wives, Blue/Orange* and *The Gods Are Not To Blame*. Recent UK theatre includes set and costume designs for: *A Good House, Torn* (Royal Court Theatre); *Jerusalem* (Royal Court Theatre); *Play On!* (Lyric Hammersmith and Tour); *Skeleton*

Crew (Donmar Warehouse); *Tambo and Bones* (co-designed for ATC / Theatre Royal Stratford East & UK Tour); *Death of England Trilogy* (co-designed, National Theatre and Soho Place), *The Corn is Green*, *Ma Rainey's Black Bottom* (National Theatre); *Richard II*, *Against* (Almeida Theatre). Opera work includes: designing sets and costumes for *La Clemenza di Tito* (Royal Opera House), *Parsifal* (Paris Opera), *Ariodante* (Aix-en-Provence Festival / Dutch National Opera / Canadian Opera Company / Lyric Opera of Chicago); directing and designing *Don Giovanni, Anna Bolena, I Capuletti e I Montecchi* (Landestheater-Niederbayern).

Music Director/Composer/Sound Designer – Emmanuel Edwards

Emmanuel Edwards is a London-based musician, composer, and creative force whose work spans theatre, music production and sound design. Emmanuel has collaborated with renowned record labels such as Sony Music, Universal and EMI. As a musical director, Edwards made a triumphant return to the industry in 2019 with the debut production of *Becoming* (Stratford Circus Arts Centre). His theatrical expertise extends to productions such as *Joe Guy* (Tiata Fahodzi/Soho Theatre), *Not Quite Gospel* (Nu Century Arts), *Finding Beulah* and *Fix Your Crown*, among others. His work includes contributions to charity projects including Christian Aid and United Sound Tracks, showcasing his commitment to music as a tool for connection and change. Beyond the stage and studio, Emmanuel is behind Oluwagbemiga, a platform dedicated to exploring the intersections of music, culture and storytelling.

Lighting Designer – Charles Balfour

Charles Balfour's theatre credits include: *Ben and Imo* (RSC/Orange Tree Theatre); *Here In America* (Orange Tree); *Summer 1954* (Bath Theatre Royal); *A Museum in Baghdad* (RSC); *The Kite Runner* (Wyndam's Theatre London & tour);

Get Up Stand Up: The Bob Marley Story (Lyric Theatre); *The Corn Is Green, Rutherford and Son* (National Theatre); *Egyptians* (Wild Yak/Gulbenkian Theatre); *The Three Musketeers* (New Vic Theatre); *Our Lady of Kibeho* (Royal & Derngate); *Romeo and Juliet* (RSC); *The Prime of Miss Jean Brodie* (Donmar Warehouse); *Frost/Nixon* (Sheffield Crucible); *Miss Littlewood* (RSC); *Against* (Almeida Theatre); *Queen Anne* (Theatre Royal Haymarket); *Romeo and Juliet* (Shakespeare's Globe); *Sadko* (Ghent Opera). His awards include: 2013 Knight of Illumination award for *The River* (Royal Court Theatre); UK Theatre Award Best Design; Broadway World Best West End Lighting.

Associate Director/Movement Director – Kemi Durosinmi

Kemi Durosinmi is a multi-hyphenate performer and creative artist working across theatre, film and television. As a theatre maker, she specialises in movement and storytelling, with work spanning choreography, movement direction and emerging practices in intimacy and fight direction. Her theatre credits include *BECOMING* (Stratford Circus), *The Little Prince* (Fuel/ETT), *The Glass Menagerie* (Arcola Theatre, Watford Palace), *The Book of Grace* (Arcola Theatre) and *The Secret Lives of Baba Segi's Wives* (Arcola Theatre/Elufowoju jr Ensemble). She is OFFIE-nominated for Best Choreography.

Stage Manager (on Book) – Naomi Shanson

Naomi is a London-based freelance Stage Manager. Most recent credits include: *WEER* (Soho Theatre Walthamstow), *The LeftBehinds* (National Theatre) and *The Guest* (Omnibus Theatre). Naomi studied stage management at the Royal Welsh College of Music and Drama.

Assistant Stage Manager – Joe Collins

Joe is a graduate of Bristol Old Vic Theatre School with a degree in Production Arts (2024). With a passion for theatre he has been entrenched in the backstage world since secondary school and has done work placements at the National Theatre, Bristol Old Vic Theatre and Jermyn Street Theatre, among others. Previous credits include: *Beauty and the Beast* (KD Theatre Productions), *Tiger Country* (Tobacco Factory Theatres), *Arabian Nights* (Bristol Old Vic), *While Shepherds Watched* (Theatre in Education Tour), *Dorian & Wasted* (Wardrobe Theatre), *Robin Hood & Marian* (Redgrave Theatre), *Loam* (Bristol Old Vic).

Production Manager – Joe Prentice

Joe Prentice specialises in theatre production and general management. Prior to *54.60 Africa*, Prentice also worked on *The Secret Lives of Baba Segi's Wives* at Arcola Theatre. His production company is called Joe Prentice Productions and most recently produced *POSH* by Laura Wade for a UK tour.

Dramaturg – Mert Dilek

Mert Dilek is a writer for stage and screen, and a dramaturg with extensive experience in major theatres in the UK and Turkey. He is currently the Literary Associate at Arcola Theatre and serves on the Reading Panel at the National Theatre in London. He also scouts new work in the UK and the US for productions and adaptations elsewhere, cooperating with award-winning creative teams to facilitate the development of scripts across languages and cultural contexts. His writing credits include *The Dreamer* (Zorlu Performing Arts Center), *The Velveteen Rabbit* (as songwriter; UNIQ Hall) and *1923* (Zorlu Performing Arts Center). His critical and scholarly writing has appeared in publications ranging from *The Stage*, *The Arts Desk* and *The Theatre Times* to *Modern Drama*, *Theatre Journal* and *PAJ*.

Associate Producer – Thomas Kell (Elufowoju jr Ensemble)

Thomas Kell was Administrative Director of tiata fahodzi (2007–15), working successively with Artistic Directors Femi Elufowoju jr, Lucian Msamati and Natalie Ibu. He was subsequently a Senior Programme Manager for the British Council and Consultant for Tangle. Thomas is the Chair of Pursued by a Bear theatre company. During 2024 he helped produce Geraldine Pilgrim's *Memento Mori* (R&D at Highgate Cemetery, London). As a musician he has accompanied Tayo Aluko for all three of his acclaimed one-man shows and is Director of Music for the churches of Our Most Holy Redeemer, Exmouth Market and St Mark, Myddelton Square, London.

54.60 Africa

A NOTE FOR THE ENSEMBLE, DIRECTOR & CREATIVE TEAM

This is a three-act piece with two intervals.

It has been conceived by the author for a near-sparse stage in which *characters, locations and purpose collide and evolve with much freedom. It is expected that all performers are on the verge of action at every given point regardless of their engagement in the ensuing scenes. There should be no 'dressing room' moments.

To achieve the above, the vision for this 'in-the round' experience is for the stage to occupy a prop-based set, with costumes and aesthetics being bold and colourful, lighting unapologetically susceptible to the mood and climate of each sequential moment.

Sound, choral and music interjections must embody an infectious and mesmeric quality. The movement vocabulary pulsating and graceful when required. We are in Africa, after all.

The conceit for text delivery is two-fold. Where the narrative is in *italics*, this indicates direct address to the audience. Where it is written in standard form, this suggests conventional dialogue between characters.

The ensemble is all-encompassing. Everyone sings, everyone moves, everyone speaks, everyone breathes. Nothing and no one dies. Enjoy.

Femi Elufowoju jr (May, 2025)

*pseudonyms used in each country, not real names, to protect the identities of individuals

Dedicated to my parents, Johnson Oluwafemi and Regina Mojoyin, for giving me my first taste of Africa. I never looked back.

A company of eleven storytellers, including musicians, singers and dancers.

Characters

Africa 1–11
Yaa
Olódùmarè
Obatalá
Tomy
Zuri
Eunice
Head Militia
Driver
Jama
Jobert
Dad
Maita
Ruvimbo
Officer
Esther
Yolisa
Brenda
Stanley
Inspector
Lofti
Sirwan
Captain
Kunta
Ruth
Memory

Act One

Scene One

Beginning

*Beginners, clearance. Houselights on. The **Ensemble** walk on stage.*

Africa 2 *addresses audience.*

Africa 2   *The story you're about to experience is our retelling of one person's journey through the entire continent of Africa. One person's journey retold by an ensemble of eleven storytellers. Us. We begin. Lights.*

Ensemble *transform into a congregation of mourners. A coffin draped in the colours of Pan-Africa appears. Musicians underscore.*

>   Bu-jumbura
>   Khartoum Niamey
>   Ouaga-dougou

Africa 7 *places Bible on coffin.*

>   Tunis Rabat Cape Town

Djembe ceases.

Africa 7   Sisters, brothers. Friends.

We are gathered here today, to witness the peaceful transition . . .

Yaa Africa   Stop!!

*From the shadows emerges a dishevelled Olódùmarè (**Yaa Africa**), accompanied by **Africa 5**, an orisha. **Yaa** collapses besides the coffin, displaces flag and lifts lid to coffin. She retrieves a staff and rises.*

Yaa Africa   Enemies of progress. You look down on me like an odious vagrant, a pariah of your shameful past. Now you want to bury me.

Friends? That which has drawn you together, who do you have to thank for that? And here you sit in croissant cafes, corporate staff rooms, multinational drive-ins without a care in the world about your real world.

This was once a space, a time when this place featured no noon or night. This world was a pool, a wide empty ocean. Man, Land . . .

Ensemble   Nothing!

Africa 6   Story story . . .

Ensemble (*sits*)   . . . story!

Yaa Africa   Time . . .

Ensemble   . . . time time!

Yaa Africa   *Time was once a living god in the sky. A supreme being, I wanted Africa to be.*

Africa 6 (*sings*)   Orisha-nla.

Aided by **Africa 10** *on acoustic guitar,* **Africa 11** *on adungu, Olódùmarè (* **Yaa** *) recounts the 'Creation of the universe' from the mythical perspective of the Yoruba heritage. Her story comes to life.*

Yaa Africa   *Resplendent in white hunter's gear, I sent my son down.*

Africa 6 (*sings*)   Obatalá.

Yaa Africa   *Gourd and pouch strapped to waist, arm, wrist amulet enabled. He was young, handsome and as he abseiled, gently floating above the surface of the sea, he revealed a hen with five toes, a pigeon and a pouch full of gold-coloured sand.*

Africa 6   Obatalá.

Yaa Africa   *. . . I charge you with the first act of creation. Go!*

*He sprinkled the soil on the surface of the water, freed the fowl.
Fowl feet scatter the soil.*

Djembe rests, **Obatalá** *dissolves. Lights.*

Yaa Africa   And that's how the world came to be. Africa,
centre of the universe, source of all things pure, wise,
compassionate.

Ensemble   Esu . . .

Yaa Africa   The devil. I can speak to that.

Yaa *staggers.*

Africa 4   Mama you are dying.

Yaa Africa   I am not dying! I breathe! And if I were to die
. . . it won't be here in this East London flea pit. Return me
to the other side. Take me home . . . Africa.

Yaa *slumps.*

Africa 10   We have time.

Africa 8   Seven days.

Africa 11   . . . to do what exactly?

Africa 6   to reset the dial.

Yaa Africa (*exhausted*)   The narrative.

Africa 2   Hopeless . . .

Yaa Africa   . . . narrative.

Africa 8   Corrupt . . .

Yaa Africa   . . . narrative.

Africa 6   Endangered.

Yaa Africa   . . . narrative.

Africa 7   We have seven days to demystify and justify
Africa.

Africa 8   To do this, all eleven of us, life-long friends, will visit the fifty-four nations in the continent of Africa.

Africa 6   *Gba be* . . . all . . .

Ensemble   Fifty-four.

Yaa Africa   Fifty-six if you count Somaliland and Western Sahara.

Africa 5   Eleven of us, everything is possible. Eleven into fifty-four anyone?

Ensemble   Five!

Africa 8   I'll do all the Ss. São Tomé and Príncipe.

Ensemble   . . . aye!!

Africa 8   Senegal.

Ensemble   . . . aye!!

Africa 8   Seychelles.

Ensemble   . . . aye!!

Africa 8   Sierra Leone.

Ensemble   . . . aye!!

Africa 8   Somalia.

Ensemble   . . . aye!!

Africa 8   South Africa.

Ensemble   . . . aye!!

Africa 8   . . . and Sudan.

Ensemble   . . . aaaaaaaaye!!

Africa 8   That's seven . . .

Africa 6   When you know . . .

Ensemble   . . . you know!!

Africa 2   You're off to find yourself.

Africa 8   I'm off to find the truth! Those cats need to see me coming. Africans to . . .

Ensemble   . . . Africa!!

Africa 9   That's huge. Seven days?

Africa 2   In seven days The Gambia turns sixty. On the seventh day we all meet there. A joint celebration.

Africa 5   . . . if we fail?

Africa 3   If we fail, we return here, bury the poor bugger, and go down the pub for a quick pint.

Ensemble   Haaa!

Africa 2   If we fail, we're in big trouble! The consequences for a collective commitment as grand as this? We would have failed ourselves, our children and our children's children. No excuse. Agree?

Ensemble   Agreed!

Africa 9   You lot have known each other much longer than I have. And you've all got roots in most of the places you're going to. I don't.

Africa 7   You do.

Africa 2   Your grandfather's tattoo shop in Maseru?

Africa 9   Not interested.

Africa 2   It's *your* inheritance.

Africa 9   In school, I was taught everything I need to know about Africa.

Africa 5   Your school produces plastic Africans.

Africa 9   I'm not plastic, I love Lesotho. But I'm not going.

Africa 4   What was your favourite subject in school?

Africa 9   Spanish.

Africa 4   Let's make this exciting. Visit Lesotho, then throw in all the Spanish colonies you can think of in Africa.

Africa 9   Marruecos, Argelia y Guinea Ecuatorial?

Africa 4   *Sí. Sí.

Africa 7   You see that curl on her upper lip? Right there! She's going back!

Africa 9   When you know . . .

Ensemble   You know!

Africa 7   I'll do homeland Egypt and the rest of the Sahara.

Africa 5   What you doing? Where you doing it?

Africa 2   Kick off in East Africa. Then Libya via Tunisia!

Africa 5   Be careful, my broda.

Ensemble   No shaking!

Africa 3   Our affirmative action is to elevate the progressive status of our continent.

Africa 8   This is not a beach excursion.

Africa 7   Objective? Gather . . .

Ensemble   Evidence, Evidence, Evidence!!

Yaa Africa   Objective one.

Ensemble   Evidence!

Yaa Africa   Strike up a conversation. If language gets in the way, you bring back that story.

Africa 5   Two.

Ensemble   Evidence!

———————

* *yes yes (Spanish)*

Yaa Africa   Cuisine. Sit down . . .

Africa 6   . . . and chop well well!

Africa 3   You run out of time . . .

Ensemble   Walk and chop.

Africa 6   Three.

Ensemble   Evidence!

Yaa Africa   Buy newspaper. There will be triumphs and turmoil on each arrival.

Africa 4   Four.

Ensemble   Evidence!

Yaa Africa   Barbershop.

Africa 8   . . . or beauty salon. Head tie; Cameroon!

Yaa Africa   Sitting in those chairs, you'll hear the most compelling headlines.

Africa 5   Five.

Ensemble   Evidence!

Africa 8   Foreign exchange.

Africa 2   CfA, Cedis, Rupees, Naira, Pula, Dinars, Kwanza . . .

Africa 3   Cowries?

Africa 8 (*humours*)   Return with cowries and I'll bust your head!

Africa 4   Stamp your passport.

Ensemble   Evidence!

Yaa Africa   . . . and take loads, and loads, and loads of . . .

Ensemble   . . . photos!

Yaa Africa   Bring back evidence of a continent worth exalting.

Seven days from now, scrapbooks full, we meet again.

Africa 3   Encounters.

Africa 8   Songs.

Africa 7   Revelations.

Africa 6   Imperfections.

Africa 2   History.

Africa 5   Politics.

Africa 3   Poli-tricks.

Yaa Africa
    Africa will probe Africa,
    Accept all hard truths.
    The severity of a crisis is ours to own.
    Say the right thing.
    Do the right thing.
    Be the right thing.
    In the names of Africa . . .
    Go!

Scene Two

Big Man

A rainswept road in Kampala, Uganda.

Africa 2   *Mackay Road, Kampala, Uganda. Three days without a local sim card. Telephone centre to the left and the MTN building on the right, offer no joy. Ahead of me is an electrical shop on a ground-floor plaza. Shutters are open. I rush beneath the awnings. Inside, behind a display counter, framed by shelves and boxes, sits the shop owner, a tall dark man who catches my eye.*

Africa 3   Come in, don't be shy?

Africa 2   *I have no interest in purchasing anything from the store. Just shelter from the rain.*

Africa 3   Step in, my friend. Take a seat.

Africa 2   *Man walks towards me, pointing to a stool. The widest grin, as if his cheeks were rigged to the diesel generator by his feet.*

Africa 3   Come in, come in.

Africa 2   So kind. Thank you.

Africa 3   Don't mention.

Africa 2   *When I sit, my head is level with his knees.*

When he moves, he leans against the counter.

I look out, the rain is relentless.

I look at the store owner, there's that megawatt smile again staring back at me. I sit.

Africa 3   You look . . *Hmm.* Do I know you? Jason?

Africa 2   *How mad is that? In the heart of torrential drenched Kampala. Only my name's not Jason.*

Africa 3   I know you. I see you from TV. You're in the movie.

I have to be right, yes. I know your face.

Africa 2   Me?

Africa 3   You've never done movie before?

It's you, yes. Wow, Oh my God!

Africa 2 *(offering hand)*   . . . Africa.

Africa 3   *Hafrica.* Nice.

Africa 2   Africa with an A.

Africa 3   Africa with an A, nice to meet you.

Tomy Zanda. Zanda is my family name.

Africa 2   Zanda Uganda?

Africa 3   Yes, it works, right?

Look at you, you're in my shop.

Africa 2   I know . . .

Africa 3   What are you doing in my shop?

Africa 2   I'm sitting on a stool sheltering from the rain.

Africa 3   Stop it!

Are you visiting Kampala or do you live here?

Africa 2   I'm travelling. Do you do sim cards?

Africa 3   No I don't. (*Changes tack.*) You shooting a movie?

Africa 2   No o, I'm travelling.

Africa 3   Traveller!

Africa 2   On a mission. Coming from Kigali into . . .

Africa 3   . . . the 'Pearl of Africa'.

Africa 2   It's God.

Africa 3   Wow!! You're in my shop.

Africa 2   I'm in your shop o.

Africa 3   Are you sure?

Africa 2   Yes now, this is me. I'm sure.

Africa 3   You're playing with my mind o. So you're from Rwanda?

Africa 2   Yes . . . no, no. I was visiting Burundi then on to Rwanda. Kigali. I live in the UK.

Africa 3   UK?

Africa 2   London, to be exact.

Africa 3   But you're African, why UK?

Africa 2   Sierra Leonean, mistakenly born in UK.

Africa 3   Mistakenly? How?

Africa 2   Blame my mama.

Africa 3   . . . but not your papa?

Africa 2   aaaah . . . I blame both of them . . .

Africa 3   Haaaaa, historian.

Africa 2   Historian? (*Whipping out a small notebook.*) How did you guess?

Africa 3   You tell stories my brother.

Africa 2   The right stories, and getting those stories, right.

Africa 3   So you board coach to Jaguar Park from Kigali?

Africa 2   No, Trinity Terminal.

Africa 3   Not coach, minibus?

Africa 2   Yes now.

Africa 3   You are brave o. Big man like you. Minibus?

Africa 2   I'm not a big man o, Museveni is 'big man'.

Africa 3 (*stern*)   Ah don't mention his name like that. You want to get me in trouble?

Africa 2   Sorry, sorry.

Africa 3   Sorry for yourself. I play with you.

Africa 2   *Ahhhhhhh.*

Tomy *is empathetic.* **Yaa** *appears, visible only to* **Africa 2**.

Africa 3 (*ponders*)   Rwanda. You visit Genocide Memorial?

Africa 2   Had to.

Africa 3   Rwanda has story. Uganda has story. But Rwandans . . .

Yaa Africa   *Dark shadows are bitter leaves of our lives.*

Africa 3   Rwandans have lived to think beyond the hurt and pain.

Yaa Africa   *Eight million people across mountainous terrain. Home for centuries . . .*

Africa 3   *. . . one people, one language, one history.*

Africa 6   Oya . . .

Yaa Africa   . . . continue.

Africa 2   Tomy this your shop, is something.

Africa 3   When you cope there is hope. You dare to live.

Africa 2   I understand.

Africa 3   You understand?

Africa 2   My home is here in Africa.

Africa 3   You? (*Kisses his teeth.*) You 'Come and go' Africa? This Africa is rooted, hustling.

Africa 2 (*taking in the shop*)   I can see your hustle is real. Museveni's last term right?

Africa 3   Me I don't look at election o.

2026. Maybe someone else will come into power.

Maybe you . . .

Africa 2   Me?

Africa 3   Aaaah maybe. Maybe Bobi Wine. Big man Museveni. He does not want to leave. Thirty-nine years and still here. He'll probably run again in 2026.

So storyteller . . .

Africa 2 (*enjoying the new appellation*)   Come on!

Africa 3   Where next?

Africa 2   Touching the Equator line, either here or Gabon.

Africa 3   Equator of all places . . .

Africa 2   No equator . . .

Africa 2/3   . . . no rainforests.

Africa 3   I gerrit! But we're the only ones talking.

Africa 2   We can but try.

Africa 3   You in the West, you talktalk nonsense! COP this COP that. And when you COP together, you hop from private jets. Háfrica! You see you. I will tell you about yourself.

Africa 2   I see you, I see me.

Africa 3   Me? No o. I'm an unlikely hero in this climate battle. Even our leaders. Their voice always the loudest. Our continent is the most endangered.

Africa 2   Our trees are the centre of the universe.

Africa 3   Centre and lungs of this universe. We hold years of human carbon emissions in our soil and trees. And to help mitigate global warming, it's our people who are forever removing enormous amounts of carbon dioxide from the atmosphere.

Africa 2   Keep going my broda.

Africa 3 *bursts out laughing,* **Africa 2** *sees the humour.*

Africa 3   We're just chatting breeze my friend. No one is listening to us.

Africa 2   So we give up now, who will protect our landscape for future generations?

Africa 3   Forget that one! You asked for sim card. I have MTN, Mango. Airtel . . .

Africa 2   You have sim card?

Africa 3   Always. In Africa, you find everything. British Airways engine, you want it, I have it here. Rolls-Royce edition, original.

Africa 2 (*almost on the floor*)   Give me MTN Uganda.

Africa 3 (*brings out a selection of cards, and puts one in* **Africa 2**'s *handset*)   Africa, will I make a good subject?

Africa 2   Mr Zanda. You will make an excellent subject.

Africa 3   Interview me. Put me in your book.

Africa 2   I'll write a book and tell the whole world about Sir Tomy Wakanda of Uganda.

Africa 3   Let me take you to my house.

Africa 2   Your house?

Africa 3   Meet my wife and family.

Africa 2   Come on.

Africa 3   Madam will dazzle you with *Luwombo na Matooke. FaceCrook? (*Producing handset.*) I no know Instagam.

Africa 2   Facebook? I will friend you.

Africa 3   Yes you will see my business. You will see my shop. That's how I get customers.

Africa 2 (*lines* **Tomy** *up for a selfie*)   I will friend you. right now. Tomy Zanda Enterprise.

Africa 3   This is crazy!!

Africa 2   *The evening continued like it would never end. And when it was time to leave, I prayed to God I'd meet the likes of Zanda again.*

---

* *Traditional Ugandan recipe (a blend of chicken and vegetables wrapped in banana leaf)*

Scene Three

Sapeur

Quartier Matonge, Kinshasa.

Africa 9 *(rucksack), joins in for a short lesson from the* **La Sapeurs**, *of which* **Yaa Africa** *plays a significant role.* **Zuri**, *a sapeur himself, gets on his Wewa, a popular local taxi, and applauds* **Africa 9** *gathering her breath by the roadside.*

Africa 4   **Bravo continue comme ça.*

Africa 9   ***Merci beaucoup.*

Africa 4   ****Ozali danseuse oyo alati malamu mingi . . .*

Africa 9 *(moving on)*   *****Merci pour le compliment.*

He follows me. I ignore him and continue walking.

Africa 4   ******yaya ya mwasi?*

Sister . . .?

Africa 9 *(still walking)*   Are you taxi bike?

Africa 4   Yes this my Wewa. Where are you going sister?

Africa 9   Ferry Beach.

Africa 4   Ngobila? Fleuve Congo . . .

Africa 9   *Charming and persistent.* Yes River Congo.

Africa 4   Ah *Fleuve* Congo.

Africa 9 *(friendly)*   *******Oui Oui Oui*

Africa 4   Ferry Brazzaville?

---

* *Well done, keep it up* (French)
** *Thank you very much* (French)
*** *You're a well-dressed dancer* (Lingala)
**** *Thank you for the compliment* (French)
***** *My sister?* (Lingala)
****** *Yes, Yes, Yes* (French)

Africa 9   Ferry Brazzaville! R.O.C.

Ensemble   Republic of Congo.

Africa 4   I will take you. **Mbongo, mille cinqsa.*

Africa 9   *Mille cinqsa?* Plenty for a bike ride. Taxi is cheaper.

Africa 4   *Wewa* cheap too . . .

Africa 9   From here to . . .

Africa 4   . . . Ferry Beach. *Oui.* I will take you fast fast.

Africa 9 *contemplates.*

Africa 9   ***Je comprende.* We go.

Africa 4   ****Tres bien.*

Africa 9   *I mount the Wewa.*

Africa 4   My name is Zuri Kinshasa. You, Belgic?

Africa 9   No no no. Not Belgium.

Africa 4   *Etasini?* America?

Africa 9 *(amused)*   No no no.

Africa 4   Ah *Londres?*

Africa 9   Lesotho.

Africa 4   Not South African.

Africa 9   People confuse the two. Lesotho is a country located within South Africa. Completely different . . . but you are right. I live in London.

Africa 4   Your accent!

Africa 9   *Oui*, Lesotho but born in London.

Africa 4   So what are you doing here in Kinshasa, my sister?

---

* *The money, thousand five hundred* (*Lingala/French*)
** *I see* (*French*)
*** *Very well* (*French*)

Africa 9   Chasing redemption.

Africa 4   . . . like Jude the Apostle.

Africa 9   Quite. Feeling like a patron saint of a lost cause.

Africa 4   Lost cause? My Congo?

Africa 9   Oh no no no don't get me wrong, I'm loving the Congo.

Africa 9   . . . the monuments,

Africa 4   *Fleuve* Congo . . .

Africa 9   *Fleuve* Congo and Congolese people.

Africa 4   *Ba Sapeur.* I saw you dancing.

Africa 9   You dance too, though. Love your suits.

Africa 4   . . . you like to dress.

Africa 9   I like to dress yes. Jackets, hats . . .

Africa 4   . . . snakeskin boots.

Africa 9   . . . *ehen!* Cane.

Africa 4   . . . the cane!

Africa 9   *Ba sapeur,* that's right . . .

Africa 4   No Sapeur in London?

Africa 9   Congolese in London, but Saper, no.

Africa 4   . . . my brother lived in Londres. Now Seychelles.

Africa 9   He gets about, your brother. They speak Lingala in Seychelles?

Africa 4   No, but he speaks good English. Every time he calls . . .

Africa 9   . . . he improves your English. Sounds like a cool guy.

Africa 4   **Se bon.*

Africa 9   What does he do?

Africa 4   In Seychelles, maybe mechanic. He loooves cars.

Africa 9   He's a car dealer? He sells cars.

Africa 4   Automobile. He *takes* cars . . . I hear he *takes* cars.

Africa 9   He *takes* cars . . .? You mean like a traffic warden?

Africa 4   Sly job, sly people. Hide in corner.

Africa 4/9 *(joins in)*   . . . then pounce on car like hyena.

Both lose themselves in laughter. **Yaa** *appears.*

Yaa Africa   Stay on task Africa. This is one of the planet's finest triumphs. You see those fashion houses, police shacks, market traders sitting in roadside trenches?

Africa 9   I see brochettes and sambusas . . .

Africa 4   *Oui oui* . . . snack vendors and street cleaners?

Africa 9   . . . bus stop lines, civilised queues.

Africa 4   . . . the same in Angola, Lagos, Nigeria. Sister, you seem surprised.

Africa 9   . . . stop, stop, stop.

Africa 4 *pulls up alongside a monument.* **Africa 5** *becomes an eagle.*

Yaa Africa   *Outside Hotel Memling, inscribed on a monument, an eagle-shaped flag, are the words* . . .

Africa 4   *Ne jamais trahir le Congo.* Never betray the Congo.

Africa 9   What is it?

Africa 4   A reminder. Leopold treated Congo as his personal property. We had no rights to land or resources.

---

* *That's right.*

Yaa Africa   Then came Mobutu. He renamed our nation, and changed everything. The only relic of our past he could not erase is the language.

Eagle dissolves.

Africa 4   My grandfather worshipped Mobutu.

Africa 9   You?

Africa 4   Patrice Lumumba.

Africa 9   Visited his mausoleum this morning.

Africa 4   L'Echangeur?

Africa 9   L'Echangeur.

Africa 4   It was built before I was born. Papa was a cement mixer. He told me when Kasa-Vubu opened the gates, thousands of Lumumba lookalikes in tailored suits, thin ties and semi-rimless glasses, hair neatly parted to one side, gathered outside chanting . . .

Ensemble   *Oui oui oui* Lumumba!

Chant dissolves.

Africa 9   Bro, a single, gold-capped molar . . .

Africa 4   All that was left of him. His broken body was dissolved in acid.

Africa 9   Left his tomb with my notepad full. Heart frail and empty.

Africa 4   You'll get over it sister, just like we will. Wherever you go in the world, whatever you face, you will never have it as bad as those who have gone before.

Yes, Ferry Beach *droite*!

Africa 9   *Merci.*

---

* *Straight (French)*

Africa 4   Enjoy Brazzaville.

Africa 9   Freedom Square, if I can find it.

Africa 4/9   . . . *Statues des fameux Congolais.

Africa 4   Look at you!

Africa 9   I see you, I see me. (*Draws him near for a selfie.*) You're a great teacher.

Africa 9 *pays fare.*

Africa 4   But this is too much!

Africa 9   You deserve it.

Africa 4 (*calling out*)   If we meet again, what do I call you?

Africa 9   You know my name like you know yourself.

Africa 4   Are you coming this way again?

Africa 9   I'll try. Lesotho next, then Banjul to meet friends.

Africa 4   Is there room in your rucksack for a Lingala wewa?

Africa 9   Plenty space *dey* (*laughing*). If I come this way again, I'll carry you. Trust me.

Scene Four

Amba Boys

Calabar, Nigeria, to Mfun, Cameroon.

Africa 8 (*rucksack*), *turns the entire ensemble transform into a symphony orchestra made up of a troop of guerrilla soldiers, mimicking the instruments to Soul Makossa.* **Yaa Africa** *hovers.*

Africa 8   *Let me tell you about a twenty-seven-year-young sister travelling alongside me to her homeland Cameroon. Eunice, young*

* *Statues of famous Congolese (French)*

enough to be my daughter, would nod off on my shoulder. She had moved to East Nigeria and was on a brief visit home to her parents.

Yaa Africa *prods* **Eunice**, *she stirs.*

Africa 8   *Whoops, she's awake.*

Africa 6   I grew up in the mountains of my hometown, Bamenda. The hilltops provided safety from the civil war. Where we are going Auntie, there are people fighting on both sides of the border.

Yaa Africa   *Brace yourself, Africa.*

Africa 6   English-speaking soldiers, we call them the Amba boys. They fight for territory. French-speaking government soldiers, resist by burning villages, killing thousands of innocent children and their parents.

Africa 8   I need to get to Mfun.

Africa 6   Border town on Nigeria side?

Africa 8   The English region, yes. Then Ekok on Cameroon side first thing in the morning.

Africa 6   Mbafe is the place to avoid. French troops hang out, ready to *pounce* on night travellers!

Africa 8 *(shaken)*   You're wrong, you know that?

Africa 6   We are safe Auntie . . . no shaking.

Africa 8   *10.30 pm. Two hours from the border.*

Africa 6   Ah . . . love the cool breeze.

Africa 8   Muddy roads.

Africa 6   . . . hate muddy roads.

Africa 8   Hate is a strong word.

Africa 6 *(humour)*   You sound like my mother.

Beat.

You don't mind if I sleep on your shoulder?

Africa 8   You didn't ask the first time.

Africa 6   In the name of the father, may our journey be one of peace.

Ensemble   Amen.

Africa 6   May the driver of this vehicle be covered in the blood of Jesus.

Ensemble   Amen.

Africa 6   We will depart in peace and arrive not in pieces.

Ensemble   Amen.

Africa 6   This vehicle will not jam.

Ensemble   Amen.

Africa 6   It will not overheat.

Ensemble   Amen.

Africa 6   Air-condition will flow.

Ensemble   Amen.

Africa 6   If death is hungry we will not be the menu.

Ensemble   Amen.

Africa 6   Halle lu,

Ensemble   Halle lu yah!

Africa 6   Halle lu,

Ensemble   Halle lu yah!

Africa 6   Halle lu,

Ensemble   Halle lu yah!

Africa 6   Wake me when we reach Ikom.

Africa 8 *Eunice snuggles up and I look out into the wet dark.*
The rain persists, driver desperate to see ahead. Windscreen steams
up, wipers struggling to match the force of the water pelting against
them. Entire bus sound asleep; rain is rushing through a gap in the
window. I can hear the tiring horsepower of the car push against
the gales. Windscreen wipers now making an excruciating
screeching sound.

Ahead of us, there's an enormous tree laid out on its side in the
middle of the road. But the closer our car gets, it becomes painfully
clear what is laid ahead of us is not a tree, but a huge man-made
barricade.

Militia Men, balaclava to hand (led by **Africa 5** *and* **Africa 9***)*
step forward, **Yaa** *intervenes.*

Yaa Africa *To every outsider, the real background to this conflict*
is never ever fully understood.

Africa 3 *Divide!*

Africa 4 *Rule!*

Africa 7 *Abandon!*

Africa 3 *Deny!*

Yaa Africa *Three squatters . . .*

Africa 4 *An English man,*

Africa 7 *German,*

Africa 3 *and French.*

Yaa Africa *place under siege a perfectly harmonious household.*

Ensemble Cameroon.

Yaa Africa *Mind-blowing madness.*

Africa 7 *The squatters carve up Cameroon.*

Africa 3 *The French grab the North.*

Africa 4 *The English, South.*

Africa 2   *Territories with different colonial legacies united under one state.*

Africa 3   *English-speakers 16 per cent, the rest French.*

Africa 2   *Do they all live happily ever after?*

Yaa Africa   *Do the maths.*

Africa 7   *Cameroon achieve Independence . . .*

Africa 3   *. . . the squatters fuck off back to where they come from, leaving a nation in an unsavoury mess.*

Africa 4   *Anglophone differ.*

Africa 7   *Francophone differ.*

Yaa Africa   *Sixty years and counting, nation implodes.*

Ensemble   *Ambazonia!*

Africa 10/11   *Hey.*

Ensemble   *Ambazonia!*

Africa 10/11   *Hey.*

Africa 6   Oya, continue!

Africa 8   *I will never for the rest of my life forget the look on our driver's face, hands on head screaming . . .*

Africa 3   My God. Criminals!! Criminals!!!

Africa 8   *Driver slams brakes, car behind swerves, then reverses before stopping at a distance. Passengers shake awake emitting a howl of fright. Driver is shaking, hands still on his head and not where they should be, on the steering wheel. We are a few metres from tree branches, wedged into stuffed oil drums. My heart pumps hard and I feel faint. I lean pass Eunice and tap the driver in the hope he resumes driving. He is crying like a newborn baby, that and a surround sound of wailing men and women makes me want to die. And then it begins . . .*

Militia Men *roll balaclavas down their faces.*

Africa 8   *No no noo. Fuck, Fuck, Fuck!*

I turn to the driver, Drive Drive Drive MUTHAFUCKER!

In front of us, are a gang of men . . .

Ensemble   *Ambazonia!*

Africa 10/11   *Hey.*

Ensemble   *Ambazonia!*

Africa 10/11   *Hey.*

Africa 8   *. . . men in balaclavas, climbing down from the blockade and emerging from the bushes on both sides of the road wielding rifles and machetes. And just like in the heist movies, the next ten minutes meets every trope conceived in cinematic history. Our driver reverses at breakneck speed, but a 'wannabe hero' behind us continues towards Ikom, towards the devil-incarnate villains. How bizarre:*

Our driver does a U-turn on the handbrakes . . . but before our car hurtles off in the opposite direction, balaclava man catches up with us and lashes his machete at my window, aiming to smash and force the door open. I freeze, and in that one moment, with steel scrapping against steel, the spark it produces lights up the hell on my assailant's face. The world at that moment stands still.

In a flash and a miracle, the driver kicks the car into second gear and pulls away just before my soggy panties soak through the passenger seat.

We drive for a mile in pitch-black silence. Flickers of light appear as we approach the village of Esabang.

We pull into a desolate side road. No sign of life. Driver manoeuvres vehicle in a three-point turn and parks up facing the highway.

We have options. We can sit, wait till daybreak, then reattempt Cameroon, or pluck up courage right this minute while we still have our lives and road trip back into Nigeria. No one speaks, not even the driver. So I make the decision.

Passage of time as **Ensemble** *slowly fall into deep slumber.*

1 am. I wake up. Everyone is fast asleep. Sixth sense instructs me to empty my pockets of all valuables, redistribute them around the car, behind the back seat, beneath the mat in the footwell. Not taking chances in case the jungle block separatists return, as now the thought of vanishing off the face of the Earth, being indoctrinated into the Amba Militia before being trained to fight the opposition was not too difficult to imagine. I check my phone, no signal. What a mess!

4.30 am. Daybreak. Rain stops. Driver turns the ignition, and we're back on to the main road to Ikom. We reach the infamous spot. The barricade has been removed by a JCB. Next to it sits a smashed-up Datsun, the heroic car that overtook us the night before. The upper frame of the front passenger side door is prised open, dried bloodstains visible on the door. Passengers look, Eunice stares, I shudder. We arrive.

Guess what, my people?

Ensemble   What?

Africa 8   When you know . . .

Ensemble   . . . you know!

Africa 8   I made it to Cameroon!

Cheers and multiple selfies being taken from and by the **Ensemble***.*

Scene Five

Turkana

Late evening. A thatch hut in Wikililye village, Nairobi.

The Cameroon transition features two female beekeepers from Kitui district on the outskirts of Nairobi, Kenya. They carry bush lanterns. They chaperone **Africa 7** *(rucksack) and local fixer* **Jama** *through an avenue of shambas. The women carry an array of meals*

on trays on to traditional mats into **Africa 7**'s *residence.* **Africa 7**
group calls his friends. **Yaa Africa** *is present.*

Africa 7   Hello.

Africa 8   Hi . . . How you dey? How bodi?

Africa 3   Bodi dey inside cloth. *°Ko iwe?* Everything okay?

Africa 8   Resilient as can be. Where are you?

Africa 7   Wikililye village, Nairobi.

Africa 5 (**Africa 7** *with Bush lantern*)   The cradle of
Mankind. Home.

Africa 7   Say hello to Jama, my fixer.

Africa 8   Hi Jama.

Africa 5   *°°Jambo.*

Africa 4   Hey we've missed you on the WhatsApp group.

Africa 2   On the road with no data. Have you been home
yet?

Africa 7   Egypt was a blast. You in Seychelles?

Africa 8   Senegal next, then Seychelles.

Africa 5 (*to beekeeper*)   Tusker please, three bottles.

Africa 9   Wait. Are you drinking?

Africa 7   Beers are on their way. Tucking into Ugali,
Chicken wings with Poussin sauce . . .

Leaf by leaf meals continue to arrive. **Yaa** *coordinates.*

Africa 8   You and food sha. You got my Shuka?

Yaa *retrieves the material from the rucksack.*

° *How about you? (Shona)*
°° *Salutation (Swahili)*

Africa 7   You got Jama to thank for that. Wearing it tonight to keep me warm.

Africa 6   Thanks Jama.

Africa 5 *spraying the shamba down with insect repellent in a spray can.*

Africa 5   At your service Ma.

Africa 8   See you soon brother.

Africa 5   Your sister sounds majestic. You know, we Masai are fantastic cooks and make fabulous husbands.

Africa 7   She's not my sister, just a good friend. So you cook?

Africa 5   East Africa, we don't play. This is my masterpiece. Mokimo Irio beans, maize, potatoes and green vegetables with roasted Tilapia fish. Ngege recipe with beef sauce.

Africa 7   Goat meat . . . surplus to requirement.

Africa 5   *Ehen*, the Mokimo is Kikuyu. This my friend (*cradling a leaf bowl in his hands*) is the tastiest red pepper concoction this side of Africa.

On cue, beer arrives, **Yaa** *delivers. They clink bottles.*

Africa 7 (*inspects room, places lantern on side table*)   Never slept in a hut before. The crickets outside are insane.

Africa 5   Bantu crickets are the friendliest this side of Kenya.

Africa 7 (*hugging* **Jama**)   And you're the finest guide on the planet. Thanks for everything.

Africa 5   *Habari ya jioni*! (*Giving* **Africa 7** *a plastic bag.*) A gift from the Itambya Mulango group you met today.

Africa 7   Oh no.

---

* *Good evening (Kikuyu)*

Africa 5   Oh yes. A book to read on your travels *Usiku mwema.*

Africa 7 (*leaving*)   Good night my friend.

Africa 5   *I sit on the bed, a thin mattress on a spring bamboo frame. No mosquito net. I survey my pied-à-terre for the night, my shamba-style up-country hotel room. The bush lantern crackles a whisper.*

Yaa *places loo roll, face flannel and a soap bar on the side table.*

Yaa Africa   *Morning rituals. Pit latrine and bath area outside.*

Africa 7   *The nocturnal sound of the crickets takes on a more rhythmic pattern. Dragon flies, dwarf frogs and critters create a pulsating symphony. It feels meditative, the last movement before morning dew.*

My childhood visits to Egypt makes this Kitui experience less of a novelty. I'd spend days with my grandfather in a small commune on the outskirts of Giza. Evenings were often spent on the patio of his cottage in the middle of a huge farmland. But here I feel vulnerable sitting in the middle of this strange rural nowhere.

I unpack my rucksack before coiling up on the bed. The lantern continues to burn. The flicker is mesmerising, and I am transfixed by the translucent vapour, the beautiful blue, yellow and white luminous glow.

Africa 7 *sleeps. Lantern dims as Turkana Boy emerges from the light.*

Africa 7   *I stir and realise I'm not alone in the room. Adjacent to the bed sits a young boy. Damn! I must have left the door open. The lad, five and a half feet tall, is barefoot, in just a pair of severely worn-through khaki shorts. He looks at me expressionless.*

Hello . . .

---

* *Good night (Swahili)*

No response. He sweats profusely and points to my bottle of water. I am shit-scared. The boy is vehement in his gesture, and as I attempt to pass him the bottle, nerves get the best of me, and it drops out of my hand. I pick it up and unscrew the bottle top. He is now sitting beside me. He drinks. Water trickles down his neck to his waistline, leaving a trail of light brown fluid against his brown skin. He is at ease and I now feel remarkably safe.

Ensemble (*whispers*)   Nariokotome.

Africa 7   *His name perhaps . . . his beautiful face bears a thick bony ridge at the bottom of the forehead, large mouth, buck teeth, and a long wide nose.*

Ensemble (*whispers*)   Nariokotome.

Africa 7   *Nariokotome leans forward and then I see he has a missing forearm, toes on his right leg severed. He laments his story, and as he does flakes of scab float from his dried lips. Nariokotome tells me he has been on a long day's journey walking from the Rift Valley through the Kenyan marshes. Dear Lord.*

The travails of his journey leaves me spellbound and captivated. At the end of it, Nariokotome is exhausted. He snuggles up to me and falls sleeps.

Africa 7   *Dawn after the night that was. I wake up covered in bites. The bed is drenched in sweat and splattered with speckles of my blood from raging insects. I look at my bloated feet sticking out from the bottom of the bed. I then remember the lad. I look across the bed. There is a depression in the mattress where he had slept. But the boy himself is gone.*

I look to the book from the women farmers. That afternoon we had strolled between two hamlets on a kilometre-long 'bush road'. Only it wasn't a 'road' but one of many dried-up streams that never regained its affluence. Walking the rest of the journey took on a new meaning as I envisage my ancestors lying beneath the sand under our feet.

The book is wrapped in shards of fresh banana leaves. I pull back the leaves, and the Kenyan shilling finally drops.

Yaa Africa (*joining* **Africa 7** *on the bed*)   *The book is the true story of the two-million-year-old fossilised remains of a boy found in 1984 near Lake Turkana, a region not far from where we sit. That gentle overnight migratory friend was the Turkana Boy. And his discovery has enabled scientists and historians worldwide today to understand the universe infinitely better.*

Scene Six

MV Aureol

Southampton. Flags from the Elder Dempster fleet (Sierra Leone, Liberia, Ghana and Nigeria) are on display.

Africa 6   I was twelve when I first set my eyes on Africa. I was on board a passenger ship, *MV Aureol*. Picture this. The Caribbeans had *Empire Windrush*. We West Africans, the *Aureol*. *Windrush* sailed for twenty-four years, *MV Aureol* sailed fifty. Yet no one seems to remember *Aureol* in the same way.

Africa 9   My school in West London had this habit. For one day only in the month of October, little fun factsheets were distributed to us in class. At the top would be a picture of a boat, an outline of the *Empire Windrush* to colour in. On the same sheet would be a short paragraph describing how the great ship carrying immigrants from the West Indies, made a big difference to the British workforce. Beneath the paragraph was space to draw a picture of our Caribbean parents. Only our parents were not from the Caribbean but from various regions of Africa. Africa was hardly mentioned, and when it was, it'll be a passing line about the slave trade.

Africa 2   In the fifties, through the mid-seventies, *MV Aureol* traipsed down the Gulf of Guinea and Atlantic Ocean ferrying thousands of young men and women from West Africa to the city of Liverpool.

Africa 6   Elizabeth II was nine years on the throne, when Mum and Dad boarded the *Aureol* to the UK. Fourteen years later, they packed their four kids and headed back home to Nigeria for good.

Yaa Africa *joins in with* **Africa 10**, **Africa 11** *and others as they underscore the rest of this memory.*

Africa 8   Fourteen nights at sea! First stop.

Ensemble   Sierra Leone!

Africa 5   Oh my. 'Sweet Salone' returnees in tropical frocks, ship's stewards and cooks impeccably attired, along the deck ready to descend the gangway on to Freetown soil. Kroo boys yell . . .

Ensemble   All hands on deck!

Africa 5   . . . followed by lowering of the anchor into the seabed.

Africa 2/5   Freetown!

Africa 5   City of tropical lemongrass.

Africa 2   So many Black people. I was too young to savour Sierra Leone's beauty and heritage.

Africa 6   Second stop . . .

Ensemble   Liberia!

Africa 7   Sun is on full blast . . .

Africa 9   The nation of timber and diamonds.

Africa 3   Third stop. Full steam ahead . . .

Ensemble   Ghana!

Africa 6/8   Tema, we are here o!

Ensemble   Akwaaba!

Yaa Africa   The only view of Africa is from the ship. Embers burn from a beachside barbeque, as Fanti fishermen knit fishing nets, and carve canoes out of trees.

Africa 2   Ghaaaaaana!

Africa 5   . . . Land of Premium Shitto.

Africa 9   Motherland for trut.

Yaa Africa   Ancestral home of all people . . . and why Africa is the core of your existence.

Africa 7   Final stop.

Ensemble   Nigeria!

Africa 6   Lagos comes upon us under the cloak of night.

Africa 8   Apapa is teeming, a sea of colourful head ties,

Africa 9   When you and your entire family are mobbed like rock stars, that's a pretty good sign you're home.

Ensemble   Af-Ri-Ca!!!

Scene Seven

Kasa

Passport control. Two officers in caps are in dialogue with **Africa 2**.

Africa 6   What kind of visa do you want?

Africa 2   Kaza visa please. *Meet Maita and Ruvimbo.*

Africa 9   Fifty US dollars.

Africa 2   *I hand over cash. Officer Maita inspects my passport.*

Africa 6   Storyteller . . . what is that?

Africa 2   My profession. Excuse me, is that a Zimbabwean visa?

Africa 6   Yes.

Africa 2   I wanted Kaza.

Africa 9   You should have said.

Africa 2   I did. Univisa. Zim and Zam.

Africa 9   You want Zambia visa. Why?

Africa 2   That's for me to know.

Africa 6   You are in Harare . . .

Africa 6/9   . . . so we can ask.

Africa 2   You can ask what I'm doing in Zimbabwe, not Zambia.

Africa 6   What are you doing in Zimbabwe?

Africa 2 (*facetious*)   It's Mugabe's birthday, I've come to light the candles. What do you think? I'm a tourist.

Africa 9   You are not serious.

Africa 2   And you two are jokers. Can I see your supervisor?

Africa 6/9   We are supervisors.

Africa 9   We supervise each other.

Africa 2   This is ridiculous.

Africa 6 (*producing form*)   Here is complaint form.

Africa 9   We will read it.

Africa 6   And if you want Kaza, pay again.

Africa 2   Pay again. I have paid!

Africa 6/9   Ah, are you calling us liars?

Africa 6 and **Africa 9** *laugh unaware of the presence of a* **Senior Officer**.

Africa 3   *Ruvimbo naMaita*!!!

Africa 6/9 (*falling to attention*)   **Shefu*!

---

* *Ruvimbo and Maita (Shona)*
** *Boss!*

Africa 3 **Endai KuLunch.*

Africa 6/9 ***Ehoi!*

Africa 2 *My passport is handed to the boss and the officers leave through an access door.*

Africa 3 What is the problem?

Africa 2 They issued me the wrong visa. Please stamp my passport and let me through.

Africa 3 Sure. (*Perusing passport.*) I like your name.

Africa 2 Yes, sir. Thank you.

Africa 3 (*flickering through document*)   All of Africa no?

Africa 2 Getting close. Getting there. Almost there.

Africa 3 Very good very good. You mention Lusaka.

Africa 2 Final destination.

Africa 3 How long are you with us in Harare?

Africa 2 Half an hour minimum.

Africa 3 Half an hour, why?

Africa 2 When you know . . .

Ensemble   . . . you know!

Africa 2 Flight to Lusaka leaves in ninety minutes.

Africa 3 *stamps passport, hands passport over to* **Africa 2**.

Africa 3 The basket of Africa awaits you. Enjoy the headlines.

Africa 2 *I snatch my passport and speed through the terminal. I hit landside.*

Ensemble Bang!

---

* *Go to lunch (Shona)*

** *Yes sir (Shona)*

Africa 2 *Twenty minutes.*

Ensemble Bang!

Africa 2 *Control tower throws its shadow over me.*

Ensemble Bang!

Objects appear from the dark, phone, newspaper, bottled drink, snack packet, Zimbabwean dollars. All tallies with flash bulbs from camera.

Africa 2 *Phone.*

Phone appears.

Ensemble Snap! Bang!

Africa 2 *Evidence!* Newspaper!

Newspaper appears.

Ensemble Bang!

Africa 2 *Chibuku Super.*

Bottle appears.

Ensemble Evidence!

Africa 2 *Mhandire* toasted corn.

Ensemble In the bag!

Africa 2 Vendor gives me *50 billion* Zimbabwean dollars in change . . .

Africa 1 . . . that's 40p in UK currency.

Ensemble Sorted?

Africa 2 Yes!

Ensemble Lusaka!

Africa 2 Let's go!

Passengers manoeuvre into seats, **Yaa** *as white Rhodesian* **Esther**.

Africa 2   *The cabin is packed with clergymen. Esther sits to the left, a Zambian bishop on the right. Esther a middle-aged white woman makes acquaintance.*

Africa 1   Esther Harrop, born and bred in York. Eloped to Zimbabwe with my husband in the early sixties.

Africa 2   *The old British vanguard of Southern Rhodesia before the big change.*

Africa 1   She's a bloody 'Dis-Grace', I tell you. Horrible horrible horrible woman. Cow!

Africa 2   *Esther is not discreet. Our flight out of Harare was delayed by Grace wife of the president, flying out of Harare.*

Africa 1   Be careful what you wish for. You voted for them. See where Independence got you.

Africa 2   I'm not Zimbabwean.

Africa 1   Are you not? What are you then, British?

Africa 2   African.

Africa 1   . . . ah British then. You know what I'm talking about. (*Cynically.*) Dubai. Dubai?? . . . it takes under half an hour to board a private jet. Not six, the bitch!

Africa 2   *Esther is a moot.*

Africa 1   A word of advice. Don't get too comfortable with the Africans. You may be Black, but you'll always be British first.

Africa 2   *To be, or what to be? Africa asks the question.*

Act Two

Scene Eight

Papagalo

Victoria. Seychelles. The heart of Mahe Island.

Africa 8 *Victoria, Seychelles. In the mix of this cultural explosion is the Cathedral of the Immaculate Conception and a Seychellois wedding spilling out onto the street. The spirit of the wedding party is infectious as I park and lean against my rental car in full tourist mode, taking pictures.*

Jobert, *traffic warden with small spiral-bound notepad approaches.*

Africa 3 Beautiful day for a wedding . . .

Africa 8 They look amazing.

Africa 3 Are you related to the bride?

Africa 8 Oh no. far from it. I'm just passing through. Caught sight of the occasion. Thought I join in . . .

Africa 3 I saw. First time in Mahe?

Africa 8 First time on the island.

Africa 3 And Seychelles?

Africa 8 First time in Seychelles.

Africa 3 You have beautiful taste.

Africa 8 Beautiful nation. And so young.

Africa 3 Young and beautiful.

Africa 8 *As in . . .*

Africa 3 Is this your car?

Africa 8 Well not exactly. Is there a problem?

Africa 3   There is no problem. No parking along Olivier Maradan, sister.

Africa 8   Is this Olivier Maradan?

Africa 3   This is Olivier Maradan.

Africa 8 (*humouring the warden*)   Thanks for that, sorry. You must be the local *Bobby* . . .

Africa 3   Bobby?

Africa 8   I better move along then . . .

Africa 3   You can't do that.

Africa 8   *The officer begins to write a ticket.*

. . . what you doing?

Africa 3   I'm issuing you a ticket.

Africa 8   I can see that. Do you have to?

Africa 3   I have already called the office.

Africa 8   You said no problem.

Africa 3   We tow your car. You park illegally . . .

Africa 8   It's hired . . .

Africa 3   Road Transport Act, 2013.

Africa 8   Okay . . .

Africa 3   We fine driver or take vehicles.

Africa 8   You mean like a traffic warden?

Africa 3   Sly job, sly people. Hide in corner.

Africa 8 (*joins in*)   . . . then pounce on car like hyena.

You guys are the same all over . . . crazy!

Africa 3   It's a crazy job, I know.

Africa 8   I was moved on twice before parking here.

Africa 3   Anywhere but in front of this cathedral.

Africa 8   Your colleague assured me.

Africa 3   Not here . . .

Africa 8   . . . and no signage saying otherwise.

Africa 3   There is.

Africa 8   Where?

Africa 3 (*pointing*)   There, in front of Chinese takeaway.

Africa 8   I didn't see that.

Africa 3   Do you like Chow Mein?

Africa 8   Not here for that.

Africa 3   Glad to hear. You're a proper African sister.

Africa 8   *The men here; evangelists in seduction.*

Africa 3   If you have moment, let me take you to *Papagalo* for the ultimate Creole experience. Sweet Potato, Macaroni with fragrant fish curry . . .

Africa 8 (*interrupting warden*)   Excuse me, we discussing fish curries now when you're just about to confiscate my car?

Africa 3   Take.

Africa 8   Huh?

Africa 3   Not confiscate. *Take*. But you can pay on-spot fine.

Africa 8 (*reaching into wallet*)   I'll pay then . . .

Africa 3   2,000 Seychellois Rupees.

Africa 8   How much?

Africa 3   You have US dollars?

Africa 8   I need to sit down.

Africa 3   You tourist?

Africa 8   Yes.

Africa 3   Then you pay online . . . ID and hotel please.

Africa 8   *I hand over my details. Passport, hotel address.*

Ensemble   Man-Fiyo!

Africa 3   . . . Man-Fiyo!

Africa 8   You know Man-Fiyo?

Africa 3   Do I know Man-Fiyo?

Africa 8   It's in the middle of nowhere.

Africa 3   But you found it . . . all the way from America.

Africa 8   UK actually.

Africa 3   Wow. To find the illest hills on the island. The crystal waters of the Indian Ocean, all from one balcony.

Africa 8   Here we go . . .

Africa 3   Man-Fiyo, magnificent view of the sunset.

Africa 8   You're not listening.

Africa 3   You sit on your veranda, relax and enjoy breakfast. Romantic (*rolling the 'r' irritably*).

Africa 8   You finished.

Africa 3   I'm finished?

Africa 8   Issue the damn ticket my friend.

Africa 3   I issue ticket. It's better this way.

Africa 8   Thanks! (*Takes ticket.*)

Africa 3   Don't mention. You have plans for rest of the day?

Africa 8   I'm going to make a complaint. Your details please.

Africa 3   Details?

Africa 8   Name.

Africa 3   Jobert Mulwemi.

Africa 3 *writes on a note pad.*

Road traffic warden. I take cars.

Africa 8   I got that bit . . . Mulwemi?

Africa 3   . . . Congolese.

Africa 8   Congolese in Seychelles?

Africa 3   You do not know my story . . .

Africa 8   I don't want to. You're a nutter, you know that?

Africa 3   Nutter?

Africa 8   . . . fleecing me dry, for parking outside a church.

Africa 3   . . . cathedral, not church. This cathedral is the seat of the Archbishop. Top security. State house around the corner.

Yaa *steps forward.*

Yaa Africa   Check your manners, sister. Hypocrisy is poison. Look, listen and learn.

Africa 8   To this joker?

Yaa Africa   He's an honourable African, the world is too blinkered to see.

Africa 3   Would you park your car outside Downing Street?

Ensemble   No.

Africa 3   St Paul's?

Ensemble   No.

Africa 3   St John's?

Ensemble   No.

Africa 3   Westminster Abbey?

Ensemble   No.

Africa 3   . . . the Vatican?

Africa 8   Not funny. *I start the car.*

Africa 3 (*sings*)   '*emancipate yourself from mental slavery, none but ourselves can free our minds . . .*'

Africa 8   Can I go now?

Africa 3   Plenty freedom in Africa . . .

Africa 3   Sister, wait! We have Black Jesus . . . Inside cathedral, like Madonna, like a prayer. We have Black Jesus on crucifix. You come, we go inside. Then cocktails at Papagalo.

Africa 8   Maybe next time young man. Next time.

Scene Nine

Moshoeshoe

African Lodge, Bloemfontein.

Africa 6   Good evening.

Africa 9   Good evening.

Africa 6   Reservation, Madam?

Africa 9   Expedia.

Africa 6   Madam. No Expedia . . .

Africa 9   Try hotel.com.

Africa 6   I cannot find your reservation, Madam.

Africa 9   Try Africa.

Africa 6   I tried . . .

Africa 9   . . . Is that a ledger?

Africa 6   . . . madam?

Africa 9   Never mind. Do you have WIFI?

Africa 6   No WIFI madam.

Africa 9   Expedia says you have WIFI . . .

Africa 6 *chuckles.*

. . . and breakfast . . . Keep looking.

Africa 6   *I keep checking.*

Africa 9   Can I use your loo?

Africa 6   Loo?

Africa 9 (*patronising*)   Lavatory . . . Toi-let.

Africa 6   Madam Brenda say only residents.

Africa 9   Okay I pay again . . . sort in the morning.

Africa 9 *presents her credit card.*

One night please . . .

Africa 6   That is problem. We do not . . .

Africa 9 (*rummaging through rucksack*)   You don't accept American Express . . . I have Visa.

Africa 6   Madam . . .

Africa 9   . . . or cash. I can pay you cash. Rand or Euro?

Africa 6   Madam . . .

Africa 9   I'll take a single room. I'm not fussy . . .

Africa 6   We're fully booked, Madam, all our rooms are taken.

Africa 9 (*crestfallen*)   You're joking. One of those room's mine.

Africa 6   Madam Brenda will soon come.

Africa 9   Right . . .

Rest.

Africa 6 (*notices rucksack tag*)   Jo'Burg, Madam?

Africa 9   How did you guess?

Africa 6   Many guests come in from Johannesburg.

Africa 9   Bloemfontein must be popular.

Africa 6   The fountain of South African flowers. This is good town.

Africa 9   I'm heading to 'Kingdom in the sky'.

Africa 6   Lesotho?

Africa 9   My parents' home.

Africa 6   Wow! We are sisters.

Africa 9   Hardly . . .

Africa 6   I'm a Basotho. I've got the hat.

Africa 9   Basotho, Basotho . . . is that still a thing?

Africa 6   Of course it's still a thing. There'll be one to greet you in Maseru.

Africa 9   Maloti mountains were my neighbours as a child. Last visited when I was five.

Africa 6   *Moshoeshoe Maseru.*

Africa 9   Not been back since.

Africa 6   Eleven languages flow between us. From Afrikaans, Northern Sotho to Xhosa and Zulu.

Africa 9   God help my children. I hardly speak any of them.

Africa 6   But you speak *SeSotho* . . .

Africa 9   A little, but please don't test me.

Africa 6   You're going home. Impressive!

Africa 9   It's a long story.

Africa 6   How long you live in Johannesburg?

Africa 9   I live in London.

Africa 6   Wow!

Africa 9   London is overrated.

Africa 6   They say plenty freedom in London.

Africa 9   Relative.

Africa 6   Is it true white people dig up roads over there?

Africa 9   They dig up roads, and sweep them too.

Africa 6   White people sweep roads?

Africa 9   Yebo!

Africa 6   You're funny . . . aah! your family will be so happy to see you Madam.

Africa 9   No family, just business. Parents died years ago.

Africa 6   I'm sorry Madam.

Africa 9   The business has new proprietors I haven't met. God this is scary.

Africa 6   Be strong. You are Basotho.

Africa 9   I never asked your name?

Africa 6   Yolisa, Madam.

Africa 9   Yolisa?

Africa 6   Yes Madam.

Africa 9   No Madam. Call me Africa.

Africa 6 (*tantalisingly*)   Hafrica?

Africa 9   Africa with an A.

Africa 6   *Yebo!*

From a distance, **Brenda** *approaches.*

Africa 8   Yolisa!!!

Africa 6 (*recognition*)   Madam Brenda . . . Soon come Madam.

Africa 8   Yolisa!

Africa 6   Madam!

Africa 9   *When she appears, Brenda is a sight to behold. She wears a black shower cap, wields a feather duster and hand towel on shoulder. She is formidable.*

Africa 8   Room 307, check out. Go!

Africa 6   Yes Madam.

Africa 6 *scurries off.* **Africa 8** *notices* **Africa 9**.

Africa 8   Hello.

Africa 9   Brenda?

Africa 8   Can I help you?

Africa 9   Your colleague . . .

Africa 8   I am manager. Yolisa cleaner. Start again.

Africa 9   I booked for one night.

Africa 8   No room.

Africa 9   I booked a month ago. *Brenda rifles through ledger.*

Africa 8   Name?

Africa 9   Africa.

A pregnant pause, a pin drop, **Africa 8** *looks up at* **Africa 9** *with incredulity.*

Africa 8   Haa what?

Africa 9   . . . Africa with an A.

Africa 9 (*handing her document*)   I've paid.

Africa 8   So you say . . .

Africa 8 *scans document.*

Africa 8   *Sanaa!* You see you?

Africa 9   See me what?

Africa 8   What does it say?

Africa 9   I know what it says . . .

Africa 8   Yolisa!

Africa 6 *from a distance.*

Africa 6   Yes Madam . . .

Africa 8   Come!

Africa 6 *arrives.*

Africa 8   Read.

Africa 6 *cups her mouth.*

Africa 8   What does it say?

Africa 6   Africa Footprints Lodge.

Africa 8   . . . and this place is?

Africa 6   African Lodge.

Africa 9   Oh dear . . .

Africa 8   Yes dear. This is African Lodge. Africa Footprints Lodge is ten minutes down the road.

Africa 9 *picks up bags.*

Africa 6   Madam Brenda. Guests in 307 ask for extension Ma.

Africa 8 (*yells*)   Get them out, now!

Africa 6   Yes Madam.

Africa 6 *turns towards* **Africa 9** *aping an apology.* **Africa 9** *is walking out of the door.*

Africa 8   Africa wait.

Africa 9 *turns.*

Africa 8   Can you wait an hour? 307 should be ready soon. It's a double room but yours at single rate. That's the best I can do.

Africa 9 (*relieved*)   *I need to find a church.*

Africa 8   Sit down. Take stress off your feet.

Africa 9   Thank you. Brenda.

Africa 8   You're from London right?

Africa 9   Yes.

Africa 8   I hear white people dig up roads in your country. (*Laughs heavily.*) God is definitely Black! Yolisa! . . .

Africa 9   *Brenda heads into the back office. Yolisa is at the foot of the stairs holding two fresh towels and a bar of soap.*

Africa 6   Wakeup call in the morning?

Africa 9   Yes please.

Africa 6   My son and I will come visit you in Maseru.

Africa 9   That would be amazing. I'll show you the old family Tattoo shop.

Africa 6   . . . Tattoo?

Africa 9   The only Tattoo parlour in the whole of Lesotho.

Africa 6 (*in awe*)   My husband loves tattoos.

Africa 9   Well bring him along too! We'll design and print 'Moshoeshoe the Mountain King' on his back, right between his shoulder blades.

Africa 8 (*from a distance*)   Yolisa!!

Africa 9   I better not keep you . . .

Africa 6   . . . if you do tattoos, you must do piercings right?

Africa 9 (*surprised*)   Piercings?

Africa 6   . . . two please.

Africa 6 *instantly becomes coy.*

Africa 9   You dark horse! (*Embracing* **Africa 6**.)

Thank you for being an angel.

Africa 8   Yolisa!!!

Africa 6 *is about to dash off,* **Africa 9** *calls her back.*

Africa 9   Wait! (*Brings out phone, draws* **Africa 6** *over for a selfie.*)

Africa 8   Yolisa!!!

Africa 6   Madam.

Scene Ten

46664

Robben Island.

Stanley *a tour guide shuts and jangles big ring of keys on an empty penitentiary corridor.*

Tourists listen attentively.

Africa 5   *The world has watches. In Africa we have time. Welcome to the Alcatraz of South Africa.*

Africa 3   *Stanley leads us through the big cell where thirty-eight prisoners, three hundred guards and sixty soldiers from the army, lived and slept. You step into yard, you are hit by blinding light. An intense heat.*

Africa 5   Look out for the 'fourth cell on the right!'

Africa 3   *I imagine each stride; a step made a thousand times and more by the great man himself. An indomitable warrior who stood tall with pride, dignity and resilience in the face of oppression.*

Africa 5   There are scales, and there are scales. We are here.

Yaa Africa   The cell of Nelson Rolihlahla 'Madiba' Mandela. In one sweet minute you'll smell the nobility of a man who for twenty-seven years, recoiled and buckled under the unspeakable. Quarry!!

Africa 5 *negotiates his way through and °opens cell door.* **Africa 3** *steps in. As* **Africa 3** *continues his recount, the* **Ensemble** *piece together the physical infrastructure of Mandela's dwellings.*

Africa 3   *Mandela's cell is tiny. A two-by-two-metre shoe box, where everything has been kept intact. In the corner adjacent to the iron-barred window rests a rusty brown toilet bucket. Opposite, on the cold concrete ground in place of a bed, is a thin, rough mat with a single layer of fleece blanket.*

Yaa Africa (*to* **Africa 3**)   Here is the foundation of your freedom. Remember this Africa. If you achieve nothing else on this continent, you have this moment to feed your soul for a lifetime. Quarry!

Africa 5   Mandela unrolled his thin bedding each night as the rest of the free world slept in turbulence. His pillow soaked and smelt of the sweat of an emancipated Africa. If this were a mere museum of walls and pictures, our human spirit would have died a long time ago.

Lights out!

° *The author adopts dramatic licence as visitors were not permitted entry into Mandela's cell.*

Scene Eleven

Ben Guerdane

Tunis Ville, Tunisia 2017. **Africa 2** *sits upright on his bed. Gets up to pick up rucksack.*

Africa 2   *At dawn I am woken by*

Africa 7   fajr,

Africa 2   *I become familiar with*

Africa 7   adhan

Africa 2   *the Islamic call to prayer, part and parcel of the ordinary lives of my Arab hosts. I have so far witnessed the midday*

Africa 7   dhuhr

Africa 2   *and the afternoon*

Africa 7   asr.

Africa 2   *As I power walk towards Gare Centrale in Tunis, bang in the middle of a commercial motor park, I watch the synchronised movement with mats, beads and the holy Quran. A peaceful nation coming together on pavements, shop and street corners.*

I'm heading to Libya via Gabes. Reach the station 6.10 am. For a Sunday morning I'm surprised how busy the place is. Tunisians can rave man. And it's Ramadan. Wow. Damn! Bare youth dem. I'm literally stepping over young drunk couples post coital, semi-comatose all over the platform.

Africa 2   *Train arrives, we pile in.*

Africa 2 *dozes off. Enter* **Yaa** *and a* **Train Inspector** *with a ticket puncher.*

Yaa Africa   *Train to Gabes is a four-hour journey. If you're a first-time commuter on this route, you'd appreciate the transition from concrete landscape to vast farmlands and divine Tunisian mountains.*

Africa 7   *My name is Chief Inspector Hammam Lif Grombalia, and this is my train. My parents named me after the first two stops. This train, their love nest, is clean and air-conditioned. Comfort class, glorified economy. Hold on, we're pulling into Kalâa Seghira.*

Africa 2 (*awake*)   . . . *Kalâa Seghira* . . .

Africa 7   *I see Africa.*

Africa 2   *I see the Inspector.* Bonjour monsieur.

Africa 7   Good morning.

Africa 2   You speak English.

Africa 7   You think because we're in North Africa we don't speak English? Habibi, I speak Arabic, French, Spanish, your language, **kula haga.*

Africa 2   I see . . .

Africa 7   You have a ticket?

Africa 2   *I produce my ticket, Inspector hands it back.*

Sorry.

Africa 7   Easily done, if you're a half-baked African and not up on your history. Africa is the centre of the world. Everything comes through us. How far are you going?

Africa 2   To the end.

Africa 7   Gabes?

Africa 2   Yes.

Africa 7   Visiting family?

Africa 2   Oh no, onward travel.

Africa 7   Onward travel?

Africa 2   Ben Guerdane.

---

* *Everything (Arabic)*

Africa 7   Ben Guerdane?

Africa 2   Yes.

Africa 7   Well no one goes beyond Ben Guerdane. Not unless you're heading to Ras Adjir. And no one goes to Ras Adjir, not unless you're heading across the Libyan border into Tripoli. And if you're not Libyan, why in the hell would you want to go to Tripoli? Why?

Awkward silence between **Africa 7** *and* **Africa 2**.

Africa 7   . . . you *are* going to Libya.

Africa 2   I'm going to Libya.

Africa 7 (*styling it out*)   Well it's been a pleasure meeting you sir. Enjoy the rest of your trip. Hopefully we'll meet again. Hopefully . . .

Africa 7 *continues down the carriage.*

Scene Twelve

Mad Dog

Ras Adjir via Ben Guerdane, Tunisia.

Africa 4   *The journey to Ben Guerdane begins gently.*

The louage is a seven-seater commercial bus.

My name is Sirwan, I am Syrian. The driver is Libyan and so are the three men in the middle.

Yaa Africa   *Our brother, fresh off the train from Tunis, joins an East African lady at the back. They are strangers but chat like they've known each other forever.*

Africa 2   *We arrive at the first police checkpoint 23 km from Medenine. Police order us out for questioning. My Comoran friend stays in the car. This is good. Much respect for women.*

Yaa Africa   *Surprisingly, UK passport gives him immunity, and is the first passenger permitted back in.*

Africa 4   *We wonder why.*

Africa 2   *We reach B'ir Basir at 3 pm.*

Africa 4   *Sitting behind me is Lofti. He lights a cigarette.*

Africa 2   *The fumes bother me.*

Yaa Africa   Don't . . . *too late.*

Africa 2   Do you mind opening the window please?

Africa 7   Sirwan!

Africa 4   Lofti!

Africa 7   Window I'm sitting next to, do we mind opening it?

Africa 4   **Wa¹ah* you can try.

Africa 7   Alright let's try.

Yaa Africa   *Lofti tries but the window doesn't budge.*

Africa 7   ***Habiba*, I'm sorry.

Africa 2   It's okay, I think I'll manage.

Beat.

Africa 7   You're going to Ben Guerdane?

Africa 2   Yes I'm going to Ben Guerdane?

Africa 4   We're all going to Ben Guerdane. We are brothers.

Africa 2   Brothers, wow.

Africa 4 *(introduces himself)*   Sirwan.

Africa 2   Africa, good to meet.

---

* *I swear to God (Arabic)*

** *Sweetheart (Arabic)*

Africa 4   You too. (*Offers a yoghurt pot.*) You like *Leban*?

Africa 2   *Leban*?

Africa 4   Yoghurt drink. You like?

Africa 2   I do like yoghurt but . . .

Yaa Africa   Humour them . . . Take it.

Africa 7   Take, swig. Sirwan, give to our friend.

Africa 2 (*takes the bottle*)   Thanks.

Yaa Africa   *The two men watch intently.* **Africa 2** *hesitates as he has no intention of swigging from the bottle.*

Africa 4   . . . Gift.

Africa 2 *has no choice but to drink.*

Africa 2   Hmmmm . . . nice, nice. Ferment. Minty.

Africa 7   Like milk, fresh milk.

They all laugh. **Africa 2** *joins in uncomfortably.*

Africa 7   Fresh, fresh.

Laughter continues.

Africa 7   You work there?

Africa 2   Work where?

Africa 7   Ben Guerdane.

Africa 2   No, going to see a friend.

Africa 7   He lives in Ben Guerdane.

Africa 2   Hmmm not exactly . . .

Africa 4   It's a small town.

Africa 7   Very small.

Africa 4   Lofti, you know how many people live in Ben Guerdane?

Africa 7   Not many, everybody know everybody. Uncle, cousin, auntie. So who is your friend?

Africa 2   She s a close friend . . .

Africa 4   Your friend is a woman?

Africa 2   Yes.

Africa 7   Your wife?

Africa 2   No.

Africa 4   . . . girlfriend?

Africa 2   No.

Africa 7   But she's your friend?

Africa 2   It's her birthday.

Africa 4   Birthday? . . . in Ben Guerdane?

Africa 2   I'm meeting her in Ben Guerdane.

Africa 7   Ben Guerdane is not party destination so why you meeting her there?

Africa 2   It's the nearest place both of us can get to.

Africa 4   Where does she live in Ben Guerdane, your friend?

Africa 2   I don't know. I'm new here. I have no idea.

Africa 7   Are you going to *Libya*?

Africa 2   No I have no intentions of 'living here'.

Africa 7   Not live here . . . Libya! Libya!

Africa 2   Oh I see. I'm not going to Libya.

Africa 7   You're not making sense. No one meets friends in Ben Guerdane.

Africa 4   Where do you live?

Africa 2 (*evasive*)   All over.

Africa 4   The city you live?

Africa 2   Currently Tunisia.

Africa 7   Where are you from?

Africa 2   Tunisia.

Africa 4   You're *coming* from Tunisia.

Africa 7   Where are you from, you idiot?

Africa 2   London.

Africa 4   . . . aaaah, so you are from London UK?

Africa 7 (*infuriated*)   UK? What UK? England?

Africa 2   Yes.

Africa 7   The fuck are you doing in our car you British pig?

Africa 4   What are you doing in our bus?

Africa 7   He's going to Libya the stupid piece of shit!

Africa 4   You have no brain! How dare you come here, in our car. You think you're going to survive this huh?

Africa 7   *Khuya, he thinks, we think he's going to Ben Guerdane but he's really going to Libya (*he laughs*).

Africa 2   Driver, can you stop this vehicle?

Africa 7   No he's not fucking stupid. He's not stopping the fucking car. DON'T TELL US WHAT TO DO! YOU FUCKING FUCK FUCK!

Africa 4   He stops the bus when he wants to stop the bus.

Africa 2 (*shouts back defensively*)   I did not kill Gaddafi!!

Silence.

Africa 4   What?

---

* *My brother* (*Arabic*)

Africa 2 (*contrite*)   Sorry.

Africa 7   What are you talking about?

Africa 4   Did he say you killed Gaddafi?

Africa 2   No he didn't.

Africa 7   Why would we think you lovely British people would kill our brother and leader the great Muammar Muhammad al-Gaddafi? Why?

Africa 2   You're making me a scapegoat for the British.

Africa 4   You're a spy!

Africa 2   I'm not a spy!

Africa 4   Snooping on our oil . . . our barrels, our airbases!

Africa 2   Why persecute me? I'm, I'm African!

Africa 7   Who do you pay your tax to you bastard?

Africa 2   Cameron . . .

Africa 4   Who?

Africa 2   David Cameron.

Africa 7 *and* **Africa 4** *are clearly enjoying the 'mock torture'.*

Africa 7   Gaddafi killer, you come into my country, into our bus, give the driver some shit coin to drive you to wherever you want. You won't get to the end of your journey, trust me. You piece of pig.

Africa 4   Call yourself African, living in the UK . . .

Africa 7   . . . where you, our brothers and sisters are fucked in the arse! You okay with that?

Yaa Africa   *He can't say that.*

Africa 2   You can't say that.

Africa 4   Why?

Yaa Africa   *West Africans suffer the same in Libya.*

Africa 2   West Africans suffer the same in Libya.

Africa 7   They have land of their own don't they?

Yaa Africa   Libya is Africa.

Africa 2   The land is Africa.

Africa 7   Oh no no no no. Nigerians are happy in Nigeria. Ghanaians are happy in Ghana. Libyans are happy in Libya. What's the problem? 'The land is Africa.' Since when? *Habiba* don't make assumptions. This is not London. Assumptions work very very bad for you.

Africa 2   *The driver pulls into a layby, and my aggressors pile out of the minibus. As they prepare to launch an attack, my head is woozy with abhorred images of the Isis Caliphate. Comoros leaps to my defence. No idea what she is saying but they spit back a warning. Breathing turns sporadic. I look to the left . . .*

Ensemble   Desert.

Africa 2   *I look right . . .*

Ensemble   Desert.

Africa 2   *Voices reverberate in my head. I am rubbish to these cats. This very minute, this very second, I'm a classified Libyan enemy. I am over!*

Then, out of the blue, divine intervention.

A military car pulls up. Comoros jumps out and informs the Neffatia security I'm in danger. The rest is easy. Firearms are drawn, Libyans and Syrian are ordered back to Gabes, while saviour and I are given an armed escort beyond Ben Guerdane to Ras Adjir.

Ahead of us, I watch Sirwan and Lofti empty yoghurt pots out of the louage window.

Yaa Africa   Africa exonerates.

Ensemble   Africa delivers!

Africa 2   I go no further.

Yaa Africa   *We'll keep the secret safe between us. He never got to Libya, but he lived it.*

Act Three

Scene Thirteen

Madonna

A road outside Chileka International Airport. Blantyre.

Africa 5   Last day in Malawi, last hour in Blantyre.

Africa 4   Last day in Maputo, Mozambique.

Africa 6   Last day in Angola.

Africa 3   Last day in Cape Verde. No shaking.

Ensemble   No stress.

Africa 9   Equatorial Guinea. Have heaps to share.

Africa 4   Last day Botswana.

Africa 10   Last day in Burkina Faso.

Africa 11   Last day in Central African Republic.

Africa 2   Last day in Mali.

Africa 7   Last day in South Sudan.

Africa 8   Last day in Senegal.

Yaa Africa   Tomorrow . . . Gambia.

(*To* **Africa 5**.) Focus on the world around you. Venture to motor parks and marketplaces. Absorb the pulse, the rhythm and pride. Africa is a wonderland that blends and part in harmony.

Africa 5   *Front of me two cheeky schoolgirls are by a barbeque stand, in line for crispy potato fries and roast spit Nkhuku. I stand behind a gentleman, an old school master in an ill-fitted blazer. He slaps his neck, swats a mosquito, reaches into a briefcase by his feet, before producing a small bottle of insecticide. He squirts the air around him. His eye catches mine.*

Africa 3   American! Smart man. *Muli Bwanji?

Africa 5   **Ndili Bwinɔ. Kaya inu?

Africa 3   Good Good. I see you from far. I like the way you walk. You have sweet stride my brother. You Jamaican? *Cool Runnings*. You have plenty ***Ndalama*. I have the right prescription for you.

Africa 5   You're a doctor?

Africa 3   Aieeeeee! Londoner!!! Yes! Yes! Yes! Doctor and teacher!! Read what it says. (*Tapping his case.*)

Doctor Kunta's Cabinet.

Africa 5   Kunta, as in Kinteh?

Africa 3   The real Kunta Kinteh. Alex Haley owes me money.

Let me show you something. Don't worry about potatoes. We have Ruth and Memory in front.

Africa 5   You know them?

Africa 3   Cheeky and clever, do I know them? My students. Right I have the precise clinical message for you.

Africa 5   I'm all ears.

Africa 3   Everything in my bag can solve all your problems. Any problem. Life, love. Love especially. Don't let me shout. I have it.

Africa 5   You have everything . . .?

Africa 3   This one brings back lost lover.

Africa 5   I'm happily married.

Africa 3   You want baby?

---

* *How are you? (Nyanju)*

** *Fine fine, and you (Nyanju)*

*** *Money (Chichewa)*

Africa 5   I have three.

Africa 3   You want more?

Africa 5   Three is enough.

Africa 3   Erectile dysfunction?

Africa 5   That will be your portion.

Africa 3   Ha, ha!! Manhood enlargement?

Africa 5   Chisos!

Africa 3   Ejaculation?

Africa 5   . . . young people.

Africa 6/9   Doctor Kunta!

Africa 3   The world's finest. These two have plenty. I have the lotion, watch. Ruth! Memory!!

Africa 6/9   Yes sir!

Africa 3 *retrieves a bottle from his case.*

Africa 3   Drink!

Africa 3 *gives bottle to* **Africa 6** *and* **Africa 9** *to swig. They oblige.*

Africa 3   Biology.

Africa 9   AA.

Africa 3   Theology.

Africa 6   A+.

Africa 3   Politics.

Africa 6/9   First class Doctor Kunta!

Africa 3   Show the man . . .

Hello and welcome to MalawiMind with me, Kunta, teacher PhD in unlikely Human Endeavours.

In the spotlight tonight are Ruth Nachipele and Memory
Hapuwani, final year students at Kalibu Academy here in
Chileka.

Africa 6/9   Doctor Kunta best teacher ever!

Africa 3   Thank you. Your specialist subjects please.

Africa 6/9   The fifty-four nations of Africa.

Africa 5   Oh yeah, let's go.

Africa 3   Ruth?

Africa 9   Female freedom fighters and head of states.

Africa 3   Memory?

Africa 6   Nollywood and Afropop.

Africa 3   And this is the first step for one of our contenders.
The start of a long journey towards winning the famous
glass *Mukombe*. Two minutes starting now.

Ruth. The oldest roundabout in Dar es Salaam is named
after which Tanzanian heroine?

Africa 9   Bibi Titi Mohammed.

Africa 3   Correct. Memory, which Nollywood actor has an
Israeli father and a Yoruba mother who hails from Ondo
State, Nigeria.

Africa 6   Ramsey Tokunbo Nouah jr.

Africa 3   Correct.

Africa 6   Movies; *The Battle of Love*, *Power of Love* and *Supa
Love*. I want to marry him.

Africa 3   Ruth . . .

Africa 9   Hit me!

Africa 3   First female President?

Africa 9   Sirleaf Liberia.

Africa 3   I'm proud of these girls. The finest brains in the world are . . .

Africa 5   Africa. They're good.

Africa 3   Your name?

Africa 5   I said it already.

Africa 3   Wow. Original. Girls, Africa will pay for your small chops.

Girls are ecstatic.

Africa 5   Doctor, your potatoes and *Nyama* are on me too.

Africa 3   Just *Nyama*? Your flute needs tooting?

Africa 5   My flute certainly doesn't need tooting.

Africa 3   I am cheaper than duty free. Where in the world can you find *Ngati*-tested Ogologi condom special?

I can't tempt you?

Africa 5   Go on then. What you got?

Africa 3   Viagra. *Mikango* scented.

Africa 5   What, Lions?

Africa 3   From the Serengeti.

Africa 5   Serengeti?

Africa 3   I promise. Tanzania's finest.

Africa 5   Okay, two bottles.

Africa 3   Only two?

Africa 5   *Ndalama zingati?

Africa 3   250 Kwacha for one, 500 for three.

Africa 5   300 for two?

---

* *How much (Chichewa)*

Africa 3   You drive a hard bargain. Bring it. *̈Zikomo Zikomo Zikomo* Baba. Thank you Achimweme. Thank you. Girls, photo with Professor Africa.

They gather for a selfie.

Africa 5   I'll be on my way. Tanzania awaits.

Africa 3   You not buying Nsomba again?

Africa 5 (*crossing the road*)   I'm good. Enjoy it for me.

Africa 3 (*calling after him*)   Africa! If you get to America and you meet Madonna, tell her to leave our babies alone.

Scene Fourteen

Fever

Corridor, airside. Juba International. Juba.

Africa 7   *Hard seats line the wall. A guard stands by a grey door. Another ushers me to an empty seat. I recognise two passengers from the Sudan flight over. They are waved in and out of the adjoining room, before it's my turn. There is procedure in place, and I need to get my story right.*

Inside behind a dusty mahogany table sits a tall, beret-wearing officer. No medals, but a soldier of some high ranking, no doubt. He examines both my passports, flicking pages with speed.

Yaa Africa   Africa will probe Africa.

Be resilient.

Accept all hard truths.

The severity of our crisis is ours to own.

Africa 2   Djibouti, Egypt, Namibia, Kenya, Côte d'Ivoire, Mali, Eswatini hmmmmm, impressive.

---

* *Thank you very much (Chichewa)*

Africa 7   Thank you . . .

Yaa Africa   *A wall clock and portrait of Salva Kiir Mayardit, the South Sudan president, falls into place.*

Africa 7   *The captain places my documents side by side at the top of the table. He folds his arms, rests into his chair, looks at the clock to his right. Then looks to his left at the portrait, before zoning in on me.*

Africa 2   Sit down.

Africa 7 *complies, leaning in to read the name on his badge.*

Africa 7   Never met a Captain before; how do I address you?

Africa 2   You don't.

Africa 7   *Captain pulls out a thick A4-size notebook from the table drawer. He picks up my passports and tosses them in. I catch a glimpse of fluffy US dollar bills desperate to escape for air. He opens up the notebook and skips through a list of passengers' names, their nationalities and incurred fines, the minimum being thirty thousand Sudanese pounds.*

Africa 2   Young man, what is your situation?

Africa 7   Situation?

Africa 2   African name, colonial passport . . .

Africa 7   I am of Egyptian descent . . .

Africa 2   Where is your 'Yellow Fever'?

Africa 7   Khartoum sir.

Africa 2   Please do not call me sir . . .

Africa 7   *Captain produces a yellow booklet.*

Africa 2   The Yellow Fever vaccination certificate is an essential travel document coming into South Sudan.

Africa 7   *(bringing out his phone)*   I have a digital copy on my . . .

Africa 2   You see, this is problem.

Africa 7   *He's not paying attention.*

Africa 2   How old are you?

Africa 7   Twenty-six.

Africa 2   *In God we believe, Shame on the ones who do less than the father.*

Africa 7   Thomas Sankara. I saw that graffitied across a church wall in Gabon.

Africa 2   Do you respect your continent?

Africa 7   Is that a trick question?

Africa 2   Don't be facetious. You present yourself as a hypocrite, induced by a colonial mentality.

Africa 7   I don't know what you want me to say.

Africa 2   The truth perhaps. Consider me a friend.

Africa 7   The love for my continent is irrefutable.

Africa 2   So you say. Pride, value, honour . . .?

Africa 7   Yes.

Africa 2   . . . sacrifice?

Africa 7   Working on that.

Africa 2   Work faster, my friend. If you value the sacrifices of your antecedents, you'd have more respect.

Yaa Africa   I warned you son.

Africa 7   I made a mistake . . .

Africa 2   . . . and your mistake has taken my office and president for granted. You think as an African you can gallivant through our gates, flash your British pounds, Euros, dollars unimpeded?

Africa 7   I think . . .

Africa 2   You are not thinking, you're talking. Only pseudo-speaking imposters like yourself do this. Do you see Australians, Americans, Europeans line my corridor?

Africa 7   No.

Africa 2   Chinese, Japanese, South Asians?

Africa 7   I bet you let them through without a hassle in the world.

Yaa Africa   Africa!!

Africa 7   *Yaa I got this.* And then you pay them billions to repaint your mosques and tar your roads.

Africa 2   Now you being clever.

Africa 7   You mentioned 'colonial mentality', not me . . . the number of times that phrase is thrown in my face. I think *brother to brother* you're being unfair.

Africa 2   Your anger has found a vulnerable setting my friend.

Africa 7   Where are you going with this?

Africa 2   My people were engaged in a twenty-two-year civil war.

Africa 7   Why?

Africa 2   Because there is a legacy that has driven us all mad.

Africa 7   You keep fighting.

Africa 2   I can only speak for my side. When we fight, we fight for what is rightly ours.

Africa 7   *The captain picks up his beret from the table and painstakingly adjusts it on his head. He takes another look at the framed photograph.*

Africa 2   South Sudan. When you know, you know.

Africa 7   *A few hours before this moment, I met for the first time the Blue Nile. A brilliant blue river wearing an elegant long dress which shudders into white ripples spanning Egypt down to Uganda, Congo, Kenya and now Sudan. Despite my roots this was my first encounter of its serenity. Sudan gifted me beauty.*

Yaa Africa   *Your only image of Khartoum or anything close to Sudan is what you remember as a child watching war films with Caine and Olivier.*

Africa 7   *So you can imagine my relief seeing a Khartoum from the skies resembling an avant garde modern Islamic city. As we floated almost silently over the Nile, the map print of the city from above had a fairy tale glow, almost futuristic with sheen.*

And now here I am in a neighbouring country. An estranged sister needing a big hug.

Africa 2   Khartoum, where you say you're coming from. I fear for that great city. It'll be no Arab spring, I promise you! And the West will sit back and laugh.

Yaa Africa   *This is not power. There is no uniform or soldier in sight. The message is not loud or verbose. The message is a whisper. A whisper from Africa.*

Africa 2   The mother of all gifts. It is up to us to turn. Look around you. We fight over common interests, oil revenues, land borders, cultural beliefs, yet we are blessed with the abundance of natural riches. Timber, iron ore, gold, silver and diamonds. Is it any wonder the rest of the world looks to this continent for escapism? Our diverse landscapes, wildlife and cultural heritages are second to none, attracting fantastic trade and tourism from all over the globe. How ironic. Solitude in Africa where opportunities exist for growth and sustainable development.

This is easy my brother. Africans for Africa where everything is one, one language, one currency, one president, one Africa. That is why I do what I do.

Africa 7   *The captain reaches into his infamous drawer and takes out both of my passports.*

Africa 2   I admire you Africa.

Africa 7   Thank you.

Africa 2   Here's your passport. I'll be holding on to this one.

Africa 7   Why?

Africa 2   . . . you don't need it. Or do you?

Beat.

Clearly you do. Take your 'saviour' passport. It's your necessary evil. You're more African than you think. You are fearless, stubborn, resilient. South Sudan adores valiant sons of the soil. But be careful out there Africa. Juba is a peaceful city. Don't bring your trouble.

Africa 7   *I head for the door before he changes his mind.*

Africa 2   Africa!

Africa 7 (*freezes*)   *I spoke too soon.*

Africa 2   Selfie?

LX snapshot.

Scene Fifteen

Home

Kunta Kinteh Island (James Island) in the foreground of the Albrede Statue.

Africa 6/8/9/10/11
   Bu-jumbura
   Khartoum Niamey
   Ouaga-dougou
   Tunis Rabat Cape Town

Africa 7   Sisters, brothers. Friends.

We are gathered here today . . .

A distant dirge pierces the air.

Yaa Africa *in colours of Pan Africa, appears fresh and renewed.*

Yaa Africa   In the eighteenth century, our forefathers were blamed for the purchase of captives for enslavement. Inevitably it always comes back to us. That we are the perpetrators of our own fate. The very best of us have all paid that price; Nkrumah, Nzingha, Senghor, Blouin, Azikiwe, Kaunda, Yaa . . .

Ensemble   Asantewaa!

Yaa Africa   Traoré.

I have walked this bridge all my life. That choral lament bears a singular message. At the end of the Gambia river, upstream I see ancestors, in multiple lines, arriving from hundreds of miles.

Africa 9   I see them too Yaa, slaves moving downriver on small sailing ships towards the coast.

Yaa Africa   You see them. You hear them. Sit.

Ensemble *sit.*

Today marks the milestone in the life of a nation. Sixty years. The continent's smallest nation and her most vulnerable. Vulnerable, like you. It was your choice to end your mission here. For this, I am glad. For how else would you have been able to compare your weakness against the strength of your own kind? You have seen for yourselves what you were about to throw away.

Africa 9 *and* **Africa 4** *rise and produce 'Chris', their rucksack and 'loyal' companion. One by one, the ensemble dip into Chris producing a bundle of books, an anthology of facts and stories gathered from each country. They are placed at* **Yaa** *feet.*

Africa 2   You gave us seven days.

Africa 8   Seven days to live and breathe an exemplary place of human progress.

Africa 7   Seven days to educate ourselves on everything Africa, and her empowering headlines.

Yaa Africa   I ask again, is it time?

I'm ready.

Africa 3   You will not die.

Yaa Africa   Is that right?

Africa 6   We have done as much and will continue. Anything.

Yaa Africa   Anything?

Ensemble   Anything.

Yaa Africa   Be careful what you wish for.

Africa 9   Please stay.

Yaa Africa   I will stay but cannot guarantee I'll be here forever. I'll remain in the vestiges of your minds. A timely reminder of what should be your eternal charge.

Africa.

Tonight, celebrate.

Rest, then refuel.

From beneath her gown **Yaa** *produces several pieces of parched paper. She unfurls each one to reveal illustrations. The first is of the Benin Iyoba Mask (Queen Mother) currently located in the British Museum. The* **Ensemble** *is now aware of the new task ahead.*

One by one, like tarot cards, **Yaa** *produces more images. The* **Ensemble** *lays them out.*

Africa 7   We know where to find them Mama . . .

Yaa Africa   Maqdala?

Africa 2   . . . will come home.

Yaa Africa   Luzira?

Africa 3   . . . will come home.

Yaa Africa   Rosetta?

Africa 4   . . . will come home.

Yaa Africa   Bangwa.

Africa 5   . . . home.

Yaa Africa   Chiwara.

Africa 6   . . . home.

Yaa Africa   Sekhemka.

Africa 7   . . . will come home.

Yaa Africa   . . . the Akan Drum.

Africa 8   . . . home.

Yaa Africa   Nefertiti.

Africa 9   . . . home.

Yaa Africa   Bronze statues.

Africa 10/11   . . . we will bring home.

Yaa Africa   The Great Star of Africa?

Silence as the **Ensemble** *take a pause.*

Yaa Africa   And when they all come home, turn all caskets into thrones. And perhaps they shall weep no more.

Brothers and sisters. Africa to the world.

Ensemble *including* **Yaa** *dissolve into the perimeter.*

The bust of Nefertiti appears in a single spotlight.

Fade.

www.ingramcontent.com/pod-product-compliance
Lightning Source LLC
Chambersburg PA
CBHW041923090426

42741CB00020B/3463